The Last Chance

for the
Church
to Love the Jewish
People

JEFFREY LOWENTHAL

WINEPRESS WP PUBLISHING

Printed in the United States of America

Packaged by WinePress Publishing, PO Box 1406, Mukilteo, WA 98275. The views expressed or implied in this work do not necessarily reflect those of WinePress Publishing. Ultimate design, content, and editorial accuracy of this work is the responsibility of the author(s).

Cover design by Brian Michael Taylor, Pneuma Graphics. 2 Cor. 3:1-7

ISBN 1-57921-099-6
Library of Congress Catalog Card Number: 98-60059

This book is dedicated to Jesus—the Chief Cornerstone, Who died our terrible agonizing death, shedding His spotless blood—and to every precious, small living stone hewn from that Great Rock. Both Jew and Gentile, together, you are the temple of God that brings Him much glory. May you soon be completed by His Spirit.

ACKNOWLEDGEMENTS

First, I acknowledge God, Who I believe has directed this book to be written. May He direct its distribution. He is the Lord over it and me.

I want to thank Joann Mangino for all her prayers for me and this book and for her sensitive heart. I thank the many others who prayed as well. You know who you are.

I thank my brother, Jonathan Cahn, for agreeing so readily to allow me to use his teaching on the Book of Ruth. Jonathan, thank you for building God's kingdom instead of your own.

I also would like to thank Jonathan Bernis, Sid Roth and Barry Segal for taking time from their busy schedules to review this book and for their comments, which are on the back cover.

I thank Brian Taylor for his design and tireless hard work in making this book cover. He is a good brother and an untemperamental artist. I also thank all those who gave me "Safe-House Stories"; some I used and some I did not. Each of you has a love for Jewish people that only God could have kindled. It is beautiful.

I thank Lynn Latshaw for her help in steering me in the right direction in selecting a publisher and cover artist and for her encouragement. It meant a lot.

I would like to thank Wendy Price for her typing, retyping and retyping of the manuscript with a cheerful attitude. I thank my "cover committee" for their tasteful critique.

I thank Barbara Fox for her many good suggestions.

And last but in no way least, I thank my wife, Diane, for her proofreading help and more so for encouraging me all along to believe it was good, but mostly for her love and thoughtfulness.

CONTENTS

PROLOGUE

In this book I relate, among many other topics and stories, a dream my son had in 1986, which in essence predicts that Israel will fight a war in Damascus just before she is attacked by Russia in November 1998. This may turn out to be exactly as recounted, or somehow it may have meaning other than what I now think. As Abraham discovered in the birth of his son, the interpretation of any vision is often the trickiest part. Also, Jonah prophesied Ninevah's destruction in forty days, which did not occur until many years later because the city repented.

Consequently, I ask that you, the reader, do not let any issue I discuss sidetrack you from the central thrust of this book—that trouble is coming to the Jewish people and to the church. Maybe things will occur differently from what I suggest. Nonetheless, I believe the Church is going to face a biblically mandated time of seeing Jacob in trouble and she will respond. And then she herself will be in trouble.

I pray that this book will be a source of encouragement, strength, and resolve to you who will most likely see these times. I believe this will be the Church's finest hour of all times. God's grace will be available to us as never before.

CHAPTER 1

THE JEWISH PEOPLE: GOD'S MEASURING ROD

Sooner or later every person comes into contact with a Jew, or the Jewish nation in Israel and the Word of the living God is waiting to spring into effect. God spoke a blessing over Abram and his descendants that He would bless those who bless them and curse those who curse them (see Gen. 12:3). In this way He has set this people and His covenant of promise to them in the path of the whole world. Will you bless or curse? And consequently, will you be blessed by God or cursed? It's an amazing law of God. The Jew is a living measuring rod of the heart of man and his words and his deeds. There is just no way to avoid it. Through the Jew, God tests whether a person is willing to value God's plan or not.

God has raised up the Jewish nation from the loins of Abraham, Isaac, and Jacob. Taken from the stock of the nations, Abraham was made the very first Jew. God changed

Abram's name to Abraham and made him the father of many nations. God made a covenant of promise with Abram: Through Abram's descendants all the families on earth would derive blessing. Therefore, this covenant is nothing less than the promise that Israel's Messiah would come and be the Savior and blessing of the world. The whole earth is being tested by its willingness to allow God to be true to His promise to Abraham.

God confirms His covenant through Isaac (Gen. 26:3–5), Jacob (Gen. 35:9–12), Judah (Gen. 49:8–10), and David and Solomon (2 Sam. 7:8–16). That covenant of promise culminates in the Jewish Messiah being Israel's king as well as the Savior and Ruler of the world from a place called Zion, Jerusalem, Israel. Therefore, every act against the Jew is an act against the established fact of God's promise to bless the world through Israel's Messiah. Every act in favor of the Jew is a vote for fulfillment of the full covenant to Abraham.

Psalm 2 predicts that the nations will rage against this covenant of the Messiah ruling from Israel. The following is God's response:

> He Who sits in the heavens shall laugh; The Lord shall hold them in derision. Then He shall speak to them in His wrath, and distress them in His deep displeasure: Yet I have set My King on My holy hill of Zion. I will declare the decree: The Lord has said to Me, You are My Son, today I have begotten You. Ask of Me, and I will give You the nations for Your inheritance, and the ends of the earth for Your possession. You shall break them with a rod of iron; You shall dash them to pieces like a potter's vessel. Now therefore, be wise, O kings; be in-

structed you judges of the earth. Serve the Lord with fear, and rejoice with trembling. Kiss the Son, lest He be angry, and you perish in the way, when His wrath is kindled but a little. Blessed are all those who put their trust in Him. (Ps. 2:4–12)

The land of Israel is set in the center of the earth, and with her restoration as a nation in 1948 she is somehow lodged in the throat of humanity. Her policies and actions are the subject of comment by the whole world. She is the Jewish nation, through which God has purposed to judge the world, both in blessing and in cursing. Approximately one-fourth of the Jewish people have returned to their Israeli homeland, but the rest of us 15 million Jews are still scattered in every nation for all the world to personally encounter, and to bless or curse. That decision is determined by the heart attitude of each person toward God. Those who bless the Jews do so out of respect for what God has decided is important to Him. Those who curse have ignored this.

It seems that every generation has its own opportunity to bless or curse Abraham's seed. Our generation is no exception. Is it a coincidence that since the founding of America an atmosphere of official welcome has been extended to Abraham's long-weary offspring? I doubt it. The nation founded on religious freedom, which refused to have a king other than King Jesus, which considered in its infancy adopting Hebrew as its national tongue, has for the most part chosen to bless the Jewish people. Israel has been blessed by America more than by any other nation in history, and abundant blessings for America have clearly followed and continue to this day, despite America's growing list of sins.

Will America maintain the spiritual wherewithal to continue to bless and protect Abraham's seed? Or will she unwittingly and blindly yield to the forces bent on destroying both Israel and the United States? We only know from Scripture that one day all nations will come against Jerusalem (Zech. 12:3). America's future is somewhat of a mystery.

I, for one, believe that just as America is a multinational, multiethnic, multiracial, and multireligious blend, so will America's reaction in the coming time of testing be quite varied. Yes, I believe that this present generation will soon be presented with its greatest challenge ever in regard to maintaining its support of Israel and of America's Jewish population, and consequently of God's promise to Abraham. I believe that soon-coming startling events and a hostile world will literally cry out for America to join the family of nations who seek to remove, once and for all, this tiny people of destiny that God has established to test the world's love for Him.

CHAPTER 2

ONE POSSIBLE ENDTIME SCENARIO

I got a glimpse into the upcoming earthshaking times back in 1986 when I was attending a week-long conference of Messianic Jews* and Christians from around the world sponsored by the Messianic Jewish Alliance of America. It was held at Messiah College near Harrisburg, Pennsylvania; and my wife, Diane, and our three young children were with me. After a few days my ten-year-old son, Joshua, had become ill with a fever. My wife first noticed Josh was feeling warm, so we left the evening meeting to pray for him and to put him and his brother Daniel to bed.

As we prayed for Josh I heard unusual prayers coming out of my mouth. I found myself asking God to bless him and use him, to give him dreams and visions. It was

---

* Messianic Jews are people of Jewish origin who have come to believe that Jesus (*Yeshua* in Hebrew) is the Jewish Messiah and Savior of the world, and who have decided to live and worship their Messiah in a culturally Jewish way.

more than a prayer for his healing. It sounded to me like a patriarchal blessing. They were words I hadn't planned to pray.

The next morning, my wife took our daughter Jamie and son Daniel to their children's classes at the conference, and I waited for Josh to get up. He slept hours beyond his usual rising time and then slowly walked out of his bedroom, rubbing his eyes, and announced that he had had a dream. After making sure he was healed of his fever, I told him I would make him breakfast and get him dressed for his class and, in the process, he could tell me his dream. Little did I know that the dream he would soon recount would change my life.

Josh said that, in his dream, our whole family was living in Israel with other believers in Jesus while Israel was attacked by Russia. He said that there were so many Russians in the attack that he couldn't even see the Jewish people. He said the Russians killed half of the Israelis and the Israelis killed half of the Russians; and the Russians took two Israeli hostages and kept them near water that was flowing upward instead of downward. And, through a miracle of God, Israel got the two hostages back and killed all of the Russians.

I was shocked. My hair must have been standing straight up to hear my ten-year-old boy describing events with which I was quite familiar from reading the Book of Ezekiel, chapters 38 and 39. This passage even says that Russia, along with other nations, would come in the latter days—at the end of this age—and "cover the land like a cloud" (Ezek. 38:16). I felt there was authenticity to Josh's dream, and I told him he was describing a passage from the Bible in Ezekiel; but he assured me he had never heard of it, and I believed him.

But what Josh told me next was even more startling. He said that he saw in his dream that, *prior* to Russia attacking Israel, there had been another war—that Israel had just returned from war in a place that starts with a *D* but he couldn't remember the name of the place. I asked, "You mean Damascus?"

I was completely amazed, scared and excited when he said, "Yeah, how do *you* know?"

I said, "Josh, that's Isaiah 17. It says there that Damascus will be destroyed by Israel. Are you sure you've never heard any of this in school or in a message somewhere?" I knew I had never told him, and there were not many cities in the region that begin with the letter *D*.

But the next words out of his mouth were the crowning blow that sent me reeling. He said the invasion by Russia was in November 1998! And that the entire world was watching to see who would win this war.

Well, I was fried well done at this point. I asked him how he knew the date. He said, when his dream started he was reading the newspaper in Israel, and at the top of the paper was the date, but he couldn't remember the day in November. I asked how he knew Russians had attacked, and he described the red flag the army was carrying with the gold markings of the Russian emblem. When I asked how he knew if the soldiers were dead, he said, "Because they were laying down on the ground, and they weren't sleeping."

How would you react? This dream was from my ten-year-old son who, by the way, was the sweetest, gentlest boy I'd ever seen. He was like an innocent lamb speaking such things that were far beyond his experience. I couldn't help but think this was God speaking, especially since his

19

dream fit in nicely with my own notions of the end times and Bible prophecy, which I have studied often.

Because of the date in Josh's dream, I felt I had an obligation to tell people. I didn't want a boy's dream to affect me so, but I could just imagine people coming to me after this dream had come to pass, upset that I hadn't told them. So I told hundreds of people. Anyone I felt it was right to tell. I've even spoken this message at Messianic conferences and in churches.

After a year of telling about this dream I was again at the Messianic conference at Messiah College, and I prayed that God would either show me to forget all about it or He would confirm it. Honestly I would not have minded if He "nixed" this dream, because I was tired of thinking about it and talking about it.

Though I believe my son's dream is from the Lord, I do not rule out the possibility that it is not, or that God may, in His sovereign wisdom, decide to delay these events for some purpose. When Jonah told Nineveh it would be destroyed in 40 days, the people repented and Nineveh was spared for many years. Although I believe these events are biblically prophesied and will occur, the setting of dates is always risky, and each reader must pray about these things for himself or herself before acting upon them. I give this word of caution, but I do believe these things and the remaining portions of this book to be true or I would not be publishing this book. Because this may unfold in a way we cannot see now, this chapter is entitled "One Possible Endtime Scenario."

The very night that I had asked God for confirmation of my son's dream, I also had a dream! My dream started with me standing outside of my house looking at a swastika that someone had painted on my garage door. The *swastika* is a symbol that was used by the Nazis in Germany to represent the regime dedicated to eradicating Jews from the earth. Being a Jew, this caused me great concern, so in my dream I looked all around to see if I could see someone running away. Then I noticed about a half-dozen evil-looking people screaming at me in fierce anger from the second floor of a building across the street from my home. This was very frightening, but for some reason I pointed toward them and said out loud in my sleep, "Bite the dust!" which woke my wife sleeping next to me.

When she said, "What was that?" I awoke and found that I was quite shaken from the experience. I looked at the clock in my bedroom, which read 2:15 A.M., and I just lay in bed praying quietly until I fell back to sleep without connecting this dream to my son's dream or to my prayer that the Lord would confirm my son's dream.

But as I fell back to sleep I began dreaming *again*! My second dream began with my pastor's mother, Yohanna Chernoff, and I seated on the ground at an intersection of two streets. We were seated on the concrete corner of the sidewalk, and I was telling her I had just had a dream that was the fulfillment of Josh's dream! As I said those words, I saw four men on bicycles come pedaling down the street from my left. There were two cyclists in the front, and they were holding large white crosses (about ten-feet high) while they rode. They were pedaling furiously to get away from two cyclists chasing them from behind with metal spears, obviously trying to kill them. My eyes were riveted onto the eyes of the cyclist nearest me with a spear. He looked so evil.

Then he spotted me and Yohanna Chernoff, and I had the feeling we were in terrible trouble, so I stood up and

21

pulled Yohanna into a large crowd standing behind us, hoping to hide there. But this evil cyclist stopped chasing one of the cross-bearing cyclists and came after us. I said, "I bind you in the name of Jesus!" But he said something demonic and kept coming at me. Again I said, "I bind you in the name of Jesus!" but he kept coming and then lunged at me with his spear to kill me. To my surprise, I grabbed his spear away from him and woke up.

I was very shaken at this point. I'd just had two very frightening dreams. The clock read 2:45 A.M. I got out of bed and went to the kitchen to turn on some lights (I'm no macho man) and started meditating on these dreams. When I thought about having told my pastor's mom in the second dream that the first dream "was a fulfillment of Josh's dream," I suddenly remembered praying earlier that day for God to confirm Josh's dream to me. I started to think that maybe my family would be forced to leave the United States due to persecution, that maybe my family and I would wind up in Israel just in time for the Russian Bear to descend upon us (not my idea of fun). But it seemed to me that the two dreams were really one dream interrupted by my awakening; that first there would come a persecution on the Jewish people and then on Christians, at least in America and maybe worldwide. The swastika and the large crosses clearly represent persecution against Jews and Christians respectively.

The words I spoke to those evil-looking people, "bite the dust," are reminiscent of God's judgment on the serpent for deceiving Eve when He said, "Dust shalt thou eat all the days of thy life" (Gen. 3:14). Dust is the very essence of this earth. It is the essence of all that is devoid of God. It is the curse of all that will be separated from God and His heavenly realm. I believe this represents the demonic inspiration behind a terrible persecution, and I believe that forces of hell are going to be unleashed upon this world such as have never before been allowed. There have been many terrible things men have done to each other, but they will pale in comparison to what is coming.

Since the time of these two dreams, I began to hear of others who believed persecution was coming, and also that war between Israel and Syria would bring about a war between Israel and Russia. Of course, back in 1986, a war between Israel and Syria was not as imminent as it is today—the situation has changed greatly. Syria is said to have approximately 300 ballistic missiles tipped with the deadly chemical VX nerve gas. She also is said to have approximately 150 mobile missile launchers. A present-day war with Syria, with such a grave threat to Israel's survival, could easily cause a massive response or preemptive strike by Israel. Isaiah 17 seems to indicate that Israel will ruin Damascus and cripple Syria, while at the same time Israel will lose her glory or reputation. Isaiah 17:1–3 says:

> The burden against Damascus. Behold, Damascus will cease from being a city, and it will be a ruinous heap. The cities of Aroer are forsaken; they will be for flocks which lie down, and no one will make them afraid. The fortress also will cease from Ephraim, the kingdom from Damascus, and the remnant of Syria; they will be as the glory of the children of Israel, says the Lord of hosts.

I believe that very soon, even prior to November of 1998, if my son's dream is true, Israel will be forced to neutralize the growing Syrian missile threat by some drastic measure, which the whole world will condemn. Damascus will be leveled. Jordan (Aroer) will be greatly damaged. Israel will win this war, but she will pay a heavy public-relations price and possibly become a pariah nation—hated by all. Even America may abandon her longstanding Mideast ally because of how Israel wins the next Arab–Israeli war. It could even be that American troops will be involved against Israel. It seemed unthinkable just ten years ago, but with the "fall of Communism" America seems to think she no longer needs Israel quite as much, and America and Russia are somewhat friendly to each other. I, among others, still see Russia as a grave military threat to America, but present American policy is to treat Russia as an ally, sharing military, space, and technological information. I'm no political or military genius, but in light of Ezekiel 38 and 39, this may prove to be quite naive to say the least.

Ezekiel 38 and 39 describe a war of terrible bloodshed in Israel. In Ezekiel 38:5, Russia is called by her ancient names of *Magog*, *Meshech* (Moscow), and *Tubal* (Tobolsk); and referred to as leading a group of many nations, including Iran (Persia), Ethiopia (*Cush*), and Libya (*Put*). Many other prophets in the Old Testament describe this same war. It appears to be primarily a Muslim war party, as opposed to an Arab war, because the Russians, Persians, and Ethiopians are not Arabic and because the former Soviet Union contains 50 million Muslims. Also, it is no secret that Russia is deeply allied today with the Muslim nations.

It is interesting to note the absence of Syria, Jordan, Egypt, Saudi Arabia, and the Palestinians in the invasion by Russia (and the Muslim nations who are with her). This seems to indicate a previous devastating defeat of these Arab nations in an Arab–Israeli conflict that most likely will closely precede the war described in Ezekiel. It is hardly

24

possible that Russia and many Muslim nations would attack Israel without Syria joining in, because Syria is devoted to Israel's destruction and would not miss a war party like this. Egypt, too, has recently been conducting war maneuvers as the region prepares for war and the Oslo "peace process" seems to have insurmountable problems. So it seems that the first war with Israel will involve the nearby Arab* neighbors, while the second war it precipitates with Russia is really with many Muslim† nations—many of which are not Arab, such as Pakistan, Indonesia, etc. Russia is in league with the Muslim nations; and with some, such as Iran, she is exchanging war technology for badly needed finances. Russia will probably be forced to invade Israel due to Muslim outrage at the outcome of this previous Arab–Israeli war in which Israel wins the war but loses her reputation.

If this is true, there will be a decrease in respect for Israel among the family of nations who already *annually* declare Israel to be an outlaw and illegitimate nation by U.N. General Assembly vote. It follows that this loss of reputation will affect the status of Jews outside of Israel as well. Isaiah 17 seems to predict that, in defeating Damascus, "the glory of Jacob shall be made thin and the fatness of his flesh will grow lean" (Isa. 17:4). Remember, Jacob was the one who left his home to flee the wrath of Esau and so I believe that the reference here to "Jacob" is not only to

---

* Arab: Descendants of the twelve sons of *Ishmael* who settled in the Middle East in close proximity to the land of Israel.

† Muslim: Adherents to the religion of Islam from Mohammed as contained in the Qur'an (Koran). There are more than fifty nations considered to be Islamic. They include the Arab nations, and many other peoples who are not Arab, and not necessarily located in the Middle East, but are in Africa, Asia, Eastern Europe, and elsewhere.

Israel, the nation, but also to scattered worldwide Jewry whose reputation (or *glory*—the word used in Hebrew is *kavod*, which means "honor") will be destroyed when Israel destroys Damascus.

So God's ancient people may once again find themselves on the run, this time not just in Europe, but worldwide. Once again another generation will be faced with the decision to bless or curse the Jew—this time on a global scale. Fortunately, if the nations again decide to curse rather than bless Abraham's seed, there is the land God promised Abraham in Israel for Jews to flee to. And it could all be set in motion prior to November 1998, and that is frightening. It looks like the whole world will be tempted to try to prevent God from fulfilling His covenant promise to Abraham. Psalm 2 says these nations will rage against Israel, and Zechariah 12:2–3 declares that all nations are going to gather against Jerusalem and be judged by God.

But before the whole world comes against Jerusalem, I believe the Arab and Muslim wars, and the hatred of Jews worldwide, will bring all the Jewish people to their Promised Land. Jeremiah 16:14–16 states:

> Therefore behold, the days are coming, says the Lord, that it shall no more be said, "The Lord lives Who brought up the children of Israel from the land of Egypt," but "The Lord lives Who brought up the children of Israel from the land of the north and from *all the lands* where He had driven them." For I will bring them back into their land which I gave to their fathers. Behold, I will send for many fishermen, says the Lord, and they shall fish them; and afterward I will send for many hunters, and they shall hunt them from every mountain and every hill, and out of the holes of the rocks. [Emphasis added]

The coming exodus of Jews from all the nations, likely produced by these two wars against Israel, will apparently dwarf the Exodus from Egypt, both in numbers and drama. And that first Exodus was something to behold! The Jewish people have celebrated that great miraculous time of Passover each year for more than 3600 years. Yet the worldwide exodus that is coming will be greater. In fact, the exodus from the north (Russia) is already well underway with approximately 1.5 million Jews having returned to Israel between 1987 and 1997. But I believe that God has declared that all of the Jewish people will be in one place again, even on that strip of land He promised to Abraham. And so He will allow the great anger of those who will curse the Jew, who will be driven to hunt them "from every mountain, and from every hill, and out of the holes of the rocks" (Jer. 16:16). It looks to me like almost all the Jews will be returning to Israel, possibly very soon.

Isaiah 17, which in verses 1–4 describes Israel's victory in a first Arab war, later tells of this second-war response from a multitude, an army that Ezekiel said, "covers the land like a cloud." Isaiah 17:12 says: "Woe to the multitude of many people who make a noise like the roar of the seas, and to the rushing of nations that make a rushing like the rushing of mighty waters!"

After Israel destroys Damascus, nations are going to rush upon Israel like many waters. This is consistent with my son's dream, which showed Israel had just returned from war in Damascus when Russia invaded. Just as my son said that Israel would defeat Russia by supernatural help from God, Isaiah says:

> God shall rebuke them and they shall flee far off and shall be chased as the chaff of the mountains before the

wind and like a rolling thing before the whirlwind. And behold at evening tide trouble, and before morning he is not. This is the portion of them that spoil us and the lot of them that rob us. (Isa. 17:13–14)

Notice that in this passage, plunder is the reason given for this war, as it is in Ezekiel 38:12: "[T]o take plunder and to take booty, to stretch out your hand against the waste places that are again inhabited, and against a people gathered from the nations, who have acquired livestock and goods, who dwell in the midst of the land." These two passages are describing the same war. Israel's blessing and heritage from God are being looted by this angered coalition of nations, but God, Who is determined to fulfill His promises to Israel, will not allow it.

Ezekiel also describes God's miraculous response to the Russian and Muslim plundering rage against Israel this way:

And it will come to pass at the same time, when *Gog* [the Russian leader] comes against the land of Israel, says the Lord God, that My fury will show in My face. For in My jealousy and in the fire of My wrath I have spoken: Surely in that day there shall be a great earthquake in the land of Israel, so that the fish of the sea, the birds of the heavens, the beasts of the field, all creeping things that creep on the earth, and all men who are on the face of the earth shall shake at My presence. The mountains shall be thrown down, the steep places shall fall, and every wall shall fall to the ground. I will call for a sword against Gog throughout all My mountains, says the Lord God. Every man's sword will be against his brother. And I will bring him to judgment with pestilence and bloodshed; I will rain down on him, on his troops, and on the many peoples who are with him, flooding rain, great hailstones, fire, and brimstone. Thus

28

I will magnify Myself and sanctify Myself, and I will be known in the eyes of many nations. Then they shall know that I am the Lord. (Ezek. 38:18–23)

We are now living in the time of swift payback. Judgment of man is near. The day of decision hurries to its appointed time. Heaven or hell looms before all six billion inhabitants of the earth because God is bringing Israel's long separation from Him to a close. God is determined to fulfill His covenant promises to Israel now. This is His time to favor Zion. However, the nations will see God acting on behalf of Israel in miraculous and undeniable ways, and multitudes of Gentiles and Jews will be saved. Those whose hearts are open and searching for God will see tiny Israel defeat a massive invasion, which includes what may still be the world's greatest military might of Russia. God will be greatly glorified! The nations who rage against God fulfilling His plan will be severely punished. Israel will again be wearied by the nations, and this time she will be forced to call upon God. America simply may not be there for Israel and may even be against her.

God is simultaneously working out His dealings with Israel as well as with all the nations. He is still using Israel as His measuring rod to "thresh the nations", and He is still wooing Israel back to Him so they will bless the nations. In this regard, I believe He is regathering all the Jewish people to their homeland so He can pour out His Spirit on and through them to bring worldwide revival (see Ezek. 36:24–28).

Ezekiel 39:25–29 describes the *aftermath* of the war with Russia and the Muslim nations of Iran, Ethiopia, Libya, and others:

Therefore thus says the Lord God: Now I will bring back the captives of Jacob, and have mercy on the whole house of Israel; and I will be jealous for My holy name—after they have borne their shame, and all their unfaithfulness in which they were unfaithful to Me, when they dwelt safely in their own land and no one made them afraid. When I have brought them back from the peoples and gathered them out of their enemies' lands, and I am hallowed in them in the sight of many nations, then they shall know that I am the Lord their God, Who sent them into captivity among the nations, but also brought them back to their land, and left none of them captive any longer. And I will not hide My face from them anymore; for I shall have poured out My Spirit upon the house of Israel, says the Lord God.

In the process and aftermath of these two wars, few Jews, if any, will be left outside of Israel and the Spirit of God will be poured out on Israel in what is known as the "latter rain"—an outpouring greater than Pentecost, because that outpouring is still raining on earth and the latter rain will come together with it (see Joel 2:23). Ezekiel 39:22 says, "So the house of Israel shall know that I am the Lord their God from that day forward." Both Israel and the nations will have a new knowledge of God because of God's hand in these two wars, and the Spirit of God will be poured out upon a fully regathered Jewish nation.

And so in His wisdom, God has set the Jewish nation up as a test for the entire world. To every generation—and ours is no exception—comes the temptation to curse the Jew. But God is waiting to bring great blessing on anyone who has ears to hear and implements His principle. Many nations are soon to learn of this phenomenon. It's understandable that the unsaved nations have not seen that God's purposes are in Israel, but it is tragic that the church has been blinded as well.

But be encouraged, because more and more the two folds—Israel and the believing Gentiles, known as the *true Church*—are going to be blended into one flock. And the world will see it. As we move deeper into the last days I believe we are going to see the interests of Jews and true Christians become one. Sadly, it will be persecution that brings about much of this unity between Israel and the Church; but I believe it has been the heart of God to bring them together as One New Man since before time began (see Eph. 2:15).

There has been much opposition to the unity of Israel and the church. Let's see why.

CHAPTER 3

THE CHURCH'S TRACK RECORD

M uch has been written about the failings of the Church with regard to the Jewish people. Since my purpose for writing this book is to encourage the Church, not criticize her, I will only say that the Crusades, the Inquisition, the pogroms, and the Holocaust have largely centered around an anger on the part of Gentiles concerning the Jewish role in the crucifixion of their own Messiah. Unfortunately, this anger has influenced the true Church as well as nominal Christians and churches. But why? Jesus Himself cried out to the Father to forgive all those who had a part in it (see Luke 23:34). And those who were against Him were only a segment of the Jewish people—mostly leaders who stirred up the people—as so many in Israel were in love with Him. Actually, the Jewish leaders were forbidden to put anyone to death under Roman occupation, crucifixion being strictly a Roman form of execution. And, of course, the Roman soldiers were as cruel to Jesus as they were to any Jew.

Peter, in Acts 2:23, says that Jesus was delivered to death "by the determinate counsel and foreknowledge of God." No doubt a reference to Isaiah 53:10, which says, "It pleased the Lord to bruise Him." So, if God planned it, and Jesus yielded to the Father's will to drink the cup of death for us all, why have there been so many crimes against the Jewish people because of it? Why have so many been so willing to punish the Jews?

Paul is clear in Romans 11 that God is not finished with the Jewish people, as some believe. Though Paul is the Apostle to the Gentiles, he says he enlarges his office to also include the provoking to faith of "them which are my flesh [the Jewish people]" (Rom. 11:14–15). Paul greatly desires Israel to be saved and fulfill her calling and destiny as a light to the nations. So where does all the emotion from the nations come from against Paul's and Jesus' Jewish kinsmen?

The enemy of our souls, Satan, can certainly read the Bible. He can see from Romans 11 (which we will discuss in chapter 4) that God has a plan for the Jewish people. He can also see that the Gentiles, who are called out from every nation, are called to encourage and work together with Israel. He has so bitterly and successfully opposed this unity between Israel and the Church that consequently the Church is living far beneath her inheritance of power, dignity, and authority, and the majority of Jewish people are repulsed by the cross and Christianity. I believe that it is Satan's *number one* agenda to prevent the unity of the Jew and the Christian. He stirs up a demonic hatred against the Jew in every age—and against the Christian, too. The Church and Israel will both need to undergo a great humbling process to discern that they together make up the Commonwealth of Israel in God's plan.

Maybe it is offensive to you to hear me say that the Church must help Jews or that the Church is part of Israel. And of course, as a Jew, it's easy for me to say. But I ask you to consider that the faith, once Jewish, will be so again by God's own design. For the most part, the Church has only seen Jewish people who believe in Jesus as part of the Church. Though all believers are one in Messiah's body, God has specific promises to Israel and purposes for her separate from the Gentile Church's calling. Specifically, Jesus is returning to rule *in Jerusalem* as the Lion of Judah. The Kingdom, originally the Commonwealth of Israel, will be restored to Israel. To see this will require the Church to yield to the plan of God, described in Romans 11, in soft and humble submission.

This is not to say that the Church is second-rate. On the contrary, the Church and Israel are two folds of a joint flock with the same Spirit beating in our hearts. Some purposes are the same for both folds. Some are unique. Each group has a blindness as to the nature of its calling: Israel is blind to her Messiah and the Church is blind to her call to birth Israel into the kingdom of God.

Yes, Galatians 3:28 says there is neither Jew nor Gentile, but I believe this refers to the next age. In this present time, God still preserves a difference in calling. Similarly, male and female are without distinction in the Spirit, but God still maintains order in gender until this present age is complete. How difficult it is to see the true calling of Israel, and of the Church, displayed in the context of daily living in each generation. There has been precious little unity to date between the two. Jewish people who do not believe in Jesus are not interested in being unified with the Church. Even Messianic Jews are divided on this issue. And the

Church has little desire for unity with Israel. Much has yet to take place before either group will accept true unity. But, if it is God's will, and I believe it is, our attitudes are all going to change—most likely because of hard times.

Economic disasters, wars, and excessive violence all have a destabilizing effect on nations and individuals, and produce an atmosphere ripe for violence against the Jew. The Church as an amorphous entity scattered throughout every nation is vulnerable to the winds of emotion that blow through the nations around her, especially during troubled times. Historically, in almost every nation where significant concentrations of Jewish people have lived throughout the centuries, when hostility arose against them they fled to a new, safe nation where it was more favorable to live. Time after time, a comfortable way of life suddenly gave way to hatred. Conditions in the new, favorable nation sometimes quickly deteriorated to the point where it eventually became unsafe for Jews to remain there as well, due to one or more of these destabilizing events. Invariably, some in that nation would blame their trouble on the newcomer, the Jew. Ultimately a spirit of hatred, and even genocide, was able to enter a nation through other wicked spirits (some always present, such as anti-Jewish spirits; and some newly arrived, such as spirits of violence). And like a fire that is fanned into a raging conflagration, Jews became no longer welcome nor tolerated.

So through many centuries punctuated with terrible seasons of destroying Jews, an ever-increasing mistrust between Jew and *Gentile* has developed. And thus, the beautiful mystery of Jew and *Christian* ministering life to each other unto One New Man has repeatedly been frustrated. It has led to a situation where most Jewish people have no idea that there is even a difference between Gentiles and Christians. Most unsaved Jewish people I know feel these two terms are synonymous. I believe this is the result of many hurts from Gentiles who *said* they were Christians. Jewish people have erected emotional barriers to protect themselves—barriers they cannot penetrate to discover that there are Christians who love them because God loves Jewish people so much, and that God has given true Christians His love.

But there have been instances where the church *has* loved Israel and to great effect. To illustrate, I recently heard of a synagogue in California that had been seriously damaged, I believe through vandalism. As the story was told to me, a church in this town felt compassion for the members of the synagogue, which was not a Messianic congregation, so the members did not believe in Jesus as the Jewish Messiah, but believed that some day a Messiah other than Jesus will come to the Jewish people. This church raised twenty-five thousand dollars to help restore the synagogue. One of the leaders of the synagogue, apparently deeply touched by this generosity from the church, told the pastor, "You're taking away my reason *not* to believe in Jesus." There is tremendous power unleashed by God when Christians show love and mercy to Jews. Because God is pouring out His Spirit, the enemy will no longer be able to stop this kind of thing from happening on a much larger scale; and this is going to have a tremendous effect on the Jewish people's salvation.

I am writing this book to tell the Church that I believe we are in the beginning of the days of this glorious mystery being revealed and fulfilled: of Christian and Jew becoming one in Messiah. The set time is coming and has already begun. Psalm 133 says:

Behold, how good and how pleasant it is for brethren to dwell together in unity! It is like the precious oil upon the head, running down on the beard, the beard of Aaron, running down on the edge of his garments. It is like the dew of Hermon, descending upon the mountains of Zion; for there the Lord commanded the blessing—life forevermore.

When Jew and Christian dwell together in unity it is good and pleasant, and the precious ointment of the Holy Spirit will run down the beard and garment of that priestly One New Man, for it is there that "commanded blessing" occurs. Commanded blessing includes the kind of power that brings whole towns to the Lord, where the great harvest of souls comes into the kingdom of God. It's the same place where Jesus, in His final prayer, asked the Father in John 17:21 to provide that "they also may be one in Us that the world may believe that You have sent Me."

The whole world in the same final generation will hear a powerful gospel from a unified Jewish and Gentile remnant acting as priest between God and the world. Multitudes will respond from every nation. No, not every single human on the planet, but a harvest so large that there could never be another like it; revival in every nation. Didn't Jesus say in Matthew 24 that before He returned the gospel would be preached in every nation and then the end would come? Christian and Jewish unity is going to propel the gospel in a way we cannot even imagine.

No wonder the devil has put such energy into preventing any real working relationship between Jews and true Christians! It seems unattractive—for now—to most of the people in each group, but it will not always be so. Even though fierce persecution comes to one or both of these groups, nothing will prevent the Father from answering His beloved Son's prayer! Maybe it is persecution from a raging world outside that will finally force and forge the church and Israel together into their common destiny, and *common-wealth*. The Church will see the vital importance of blessing the Jewish people, of helping God bring to birth His covenant promises to her. And in the process the commanded blessing of unity and purity will bring about Jesus' spotless bride (see Eph. 5:27). It is here that the full blessings of Abraham will come upon the Gentiles (see Gal. 3:14).

But these blessings are not automatically given to each and every Gentile. They have been made available by God to those who choose to receive them through the Jewish Messiah, Jesus, and through a love for the Jewish people. But it is becoming very clear that the Church now has one last chance in these final years before Jesus' return to choose to love the Jewish people.

Now let's see the biblical framework for the joining of Israel and the church.

CHAPTER 4

THE OLIVE TREE
OF THE FAITH

R omans 11 is probably the most central chapter of the
Bible regarding the model for how the church and Israel are to relate to one another. Over the course of my
twenty-three years as a believer in *Yeshua* (Jesus) I have not
met many Christians who have studied this chapter of the
Bible very deeply. This needs to be done, for there is a grave
warning to the church as well as a glorious revelation of
God's will and plan for the two folds of His flock that He
loves so much. If we know through biblical promise the
track God has laid, we will enjoy much success establish-
ing our railroad there, even though the majority of people
may be uninterested. If we build our railway to other places
where God is not going, we may have some success and
blessing since God loves us and never leaves us, but it will
not compare to being a part of God's plan; and He will definitely raise up someone else to fulfill His will. With that as
a build up, let's look at this beautiful portion of Scripture.

Verses 1 through 10 set forth that God is not finished with Israel. "God has not cast away His people which He foreknew" (Rom. 11:2). Believe it or not, this simple understanding that God has a distinct, eternal plan for the Jewish people could have spared the lives of countless Jews, who were considered by many established Church leaders to be forsaken by God—His enemies to be mistreated at will because God was so angry with them that killing them would actually please God. (A little study of history will bear this out.) But God never stopped wanting to fulfill His covenant promises to Abraham upon the Jewish people. How ironic that He has selected this same Church to pour those blessings upon Israel, to stir them to accept their eternal destiny to be a light to the nations.

Paul, the Apostle to the Gentiles, in Romans 11 is explaining that some Jewish people have obtained the knowledge of their Messiah unto salvation by grace, but the rest were blinded by God so that "salvation is come unto the Gentiles to provoke them to jealousy" (Rom. 11:11). Yes, it's incredible. God is saying that only a small portion of Israel was permitted to believe in Jesus through a direct revelation or through a Jewish presentation of the gospel, and the rest had their eyes darkened. Not so that they would fall and be lost, but so that they would believe through the agency of gentile believers. God has had mercy on Gentiles so they could provoke Israel to jealousy. And for this reason the glorious gospel was given to the Gentiles. The very mercy He invested in the church is to be reinvested by them in the Jewish people. God's plan is to call out a nation of Gentiles from among every nation to make Israel jealous (see Deut. 32:21). Why? So that they would spend a miserable life envying those lucky Gentiles whom God had blessed? Of course not! Their jealousy is so they would want their own Messiah because of how good He looked in the lives of Gentiles. It is given by God to the Gentiles to bring the Jewish people to Him, but until that time, the Gentiles are charged with the primary stewardship of the good news to *all* who are being saved, both Jew and Gentile.

To illustrate, imagine a lonely young woman. Beautiful, but lonely. She would like to be married, but has not found anyone interesting that meets her requirements. Along comes her best friend, who begins to tell her of the most wonderful man she has just met and married. Her life was once so miserable, but her new husband has been so wonderful that she's been literally transformed from a selfish woman to a loving, giving, caring, and fulfilled person due to the glorious example her husband has been. What's more, he's handsome and rich! That is the way it is supposed to work. Israel is supposed to see that her own Messiah and Savior has saved someone else, and learn about Him from the Gentiles in word and deed.

Sadly, the church has not always stuck to the script of Romans 11, but has done some adlibbing. However, where individual Gentile believers have followed this plan of God and patiently loved Jewish people, many have been won to the Lord. I and most of the other Jewish believers I know have come to the Lord through Gentiles! As a result, hundreds of thousands of Messianic Jews are now plugged back into their Olive Tree and laboring in the present endtime harvest.

Why would God set up a system like this? I don't exactly know. "He's God and we're not" is the best I can come up with, and that's what Paul concludes as well: "O the depth of the riches both of the wisdom and the knowledge of God! How unsearchable are His judgments and His ways past finding out!" (Rom. 11:32).

Paul tells the Gentiles, "Even so these [Israel] also have now been disobedient, that through the mercy shown you [Gentiles] they also may obtain mercy. For God has committed them all [Jew and Gentile] to disobedience, that He might have mercy on all" (Rom. 11:31–32).

So it has to do with God having mercy on all of us, first to the Jew who received a relationship with God—the promise of the Messiah through Abraham—and the first opportunity to carry the gospel as a national calling. But with Israel's national rejection of that calling to be a light to the nations, the Gentiles were shown mercy. They were offered faith in Jesus and given a calling to carry the gospel almost all alone for a time, *and* they were given the calling to bring Israel back to their God. Israel's calling was not taken away from them by God and handed to the Church as some have thought and still think. The church is to love Israel into accepting her original calling.

Romans 11:17–21 says:

> And if some of the branches [Israel] were broken off, and you [Gentiles], being a wild olive tree, were grafted in among them, and with them became a partaker of the root and fatness of the olive tree, do not boast against the branches [the Jewish believers]. But if you do boast, remember that you do not support the root, but the root supports you. You will say then, "Branches were broken off that I might be grafted in." Well said. Because of unbelief they were broken off, and you stand by faith. Do not be haughty, but fear. For if God did not spare the natural branches [Jewish unbelievers], He may not spare you either.

The Church is supposed to be grafted into Israel's Olive Tree of faith. The Church was not given a new faith tree. The Church was called out from a different Olive Tree altogether. Her tree was wild and independent, growing on its own in every nation, as we might see a tree in a forest no one seems to have planted. God has taken of those wild branches and plugged them into the spiritual heritage of Israel in the place of those blinded among the Jewish people. Not for the purpose of replacing them, but for those broken-off Jewish branches to see the beauty of being part of her own Olive Tree and to ask to come in to it so God can have mercy.

And there's a warning here: If God did not spare those Jewish people who refused to believe in Jesus, He may not spare you who are enjoying their Olive Tree of faith. So don't boast above them. You see, this is a tree of faith, the roots of which go back to that first Jew, Abraham, the father of faith. God does not intend the Church to forget or lose those roots to establish a new tree without roots. Rather the blessings of Abraham's Jewish faith roots have come to believing Gentiles as well as Jews together in the Olive Tree. Boasting above the broken-off branches is a sin against God, as is all such boasting (see James 4:16). But this boasting is also a dangerous open door that will injure the faith of the Church, for Paul warns of not being spared. Since this is a tree of faith, there's no room for boasting or pride, which is not of dependence and faith. The Ephesians are told that faith is a gift, lest any man should boast (see Eph. 2:9).

Even further, the church is not to boast *above* the branches. That is, in her relationship to Israel (the Jewish people) there must not be a lifting up over them, even though the true Church is saved and Israel is now mostly unsaved.

Firstly, it is he who "endures to the end" who is saved (see Mark 13:13). But also, there's the matter of this difficult humility and supplication we talked about in Chapter 1. Is the Church willing to see herself as grafted in among the Jewish branches? Throughout the church age, she has not seen herself this way. Even as I write this it seems to me a hard pill for the Church to swallow: A billion Gentiles who call themselves Christian on our planet somehow humbly paying respect and homage to a remnant from among eighteen million Jews, the vast majority of which are presently blinded to their own Messiah. Of course only a remnant of the Church may do this, but it is an awesome thought, and our God is awesome. He doesn't think like we do: He uses the foolish and undesirable things to wound and defeat our pride.

But the warning continues:

> Therefore consider the goodness and severity of God: on those who fell, severity; but toward you, goodness, if you continue in His goodness. Otherwise you also will be cut off. And they also, if they do not continue in unbelief, will be grafted in, for God is able to graft them in again. For if you were cut out of the olive tree which is wild by nature, and were grafted contrary to nature into a cultivated olive tree, how much more will these, who are natural branches, be grafted into their own olive tree? (Rom. 11:22–24)

So the Church is cautioned to continue in God's goodness, which is not a place of boasting but of mercy and unmerited favor. And in this passage there is a hint—really a strong suggestion—that Israel will be grafted back into faith, "for God is able to graft them in again." Hallelujah!

There it is. The plan of God. His railroad track laid before our very eyes. It's so simple yet we've missed it in large part for almost 2,000 years. Israel has been partially blinded to her Messiah, and the Church has been partially blinded to this aspect of her calling. The church, grown to more than fifty times the size of Israel, is supposed to humble herself out of loving gratitude for the goodness and grace of God, with respect for the patriarch Abraham's roots of faith and for his descendants, whom to bless means blessing and whom to curse means cursing. In this way the church will be able to see her primary calling and focus in service to her Lord in the provoking to faith of the Jewish people.

Am I disqualified from saying this because I myself am a Jew? I hope not. But I must confess, I stagger a bit at what it will take to bring this about: a huge and, in many ways, staid Church bowing low to serve God by reaching out to the Jewish people. A Church so in love with God that she will gladly choose, as did Moses, to suffer with the people of God rather than to enjoy the pleasures of this world (see Heb. 11:24–27). I know whatever God needs to do to bring the Church to this place of humility is worth it, but it surely has not happened in 2,000 years. Can we imagine the level of Holy Spirit anointing required for such humility? Maybe this is the level of anointing of Pentecost (*Shavuot*), the revival led by the apostles in Acts 2 and following.

I believe that to bring about this type of submission of her will, the Church is going to receive even *more* of God's power and grace than what was poured out in those initial days of faith on the first Messianic Jews and later in Acts chapter 8 on the Samaritans and then in Acts chapter 10 on the Gentiles. The Book of Joel, which is a chronology of the end times, in prophesying the anointing of the Holy

Spirit being poured out on all flesh (which only *began* at Pentecost), says: "Be glad then you children of Zion and rejoice in the Lord your God, for He has given you the former rain moderately [Pentecost] and He will cause to come down for you the rain, the former rain [Pentecost] and the latter rain [final days' outpouring of world revival] in the first month" (Joel 2:23). So we see a massive release of God's power is coming upon us.

And it's important to note that while this outpouring is taking place there will be birth pangs of wars with Israel and other events raining down on the earth. They will culminate in God "gathering all nations against Jerusalem" to punish the nations for their wrong toward Him and toward Israel—for cursing her and even stealing her heritage that God promised to give her. The world will be judged for its crimes against the Church as well, for she is God's chosen along with Israel. What an awesome and fearful time that is coming. It's definitely not for the faint of heart, though. May God strengthen us in it to act in a manner worthy of His great name and all that He has done for us.

It is in this context of great upheavals and great outpourings of the Holy Spirit that the Church, or at least a significant portion of those who profess to know Jesus, is going to heed Paul's message of Romans 11. Paul sums up this great plan of God to bring Israel to the fullness of faith through the Gentiles, saying:

> For I do not desire, brethren, that you should be ignorant of this mystery, lest you should be wise in your own opinion, that blindness in part has happened to Israel until the *fullness of the Gentiles* has come in. And so all Israel will be saved, as it is written: The Deliverer will come out of Zion, and He will turn away ungodliness

from Jacob; *for this is My covenant with them*, when I take away their sins. Concerning the gospel they are enemies for your sake, but concerning the election they are beloved for the sake of the Father. For the gifts and the calling of God are irrevocable. For as you were once disobedient to God, yet have now obtained mercy through their disobedience, even so these also have not been disobedient, that through the mercy shown you they also may obtain mercy. For God has committed them all to disobedience, that He might have mercy on all. (Rom. 11:25–32; emphasis added)

The "fullness of the Gentiles" is often referred to as the time when the last Gentile is saved before the rapture of the Church and then God begins dealing with Israel in the time of "Jacob's trouble" (see Jer. 30:7). It is possible that the trust of the gospel to Gentiles has a finishing point or fullness that could be measured in numbers of people saved from among the nations. However, that does not mean there will be no more Gentiles saved once Israel takes up the gospel or that the church will be gone from the earth at that point. I believe the church should prepare to be here until the last day, the Resurrection Day. Then, if there's a prior rapture, all well and good; but if the church puts her trust in a rapture prior to the Resurrection and is not spiritually and mentally prepared for tribulation and she must wait, she will be shaken.

What comes to mind is Jesus' discussion with Martha in John 11 after Lazarus had died. Martha tells Jesus, "Lord, if You had been here, my brother would not have died" (John 11:4). When Jesus tells her not to worry that Lazarus will rise again, Martha declares without rebuke from Jesus, "I know that he will rise again in the resurrection at the last

49

day." Martha doesn't say that Lazarus will rise in the pre-tribulation rapture, but on the *last day*. She may have learned this from Jesus' message in John 6 where Jesus says no less than four times (vss. 39, 40, 44, 54) that He will raise up on "the last day" those who believe in Him. Put this together with Paul's explanation in 1 Thessalonians 4:14–17, which states:

> For if we believe that Jesus died and rose again, even so God will bring with Him those who sleep in Jesus. For this we say to you by the word of the Lord, that we who are alive and remain until the coming of the Lord will by no means precede those who are asleep. For the Lord Himself will descend from heaven with a shout, with the voice of an archangel, and with the trumpet of God. And the dead in Christ will rise first. Then we who are alive and remain shall be caught up together with them in the clouds to meet the Lord in the air. And thus we shall always be with the Lord.

It seems quite plausible that we who are alive and remain will be caught up on the last day of this age with those who have already died in Messiah. That includes every believer in Jesus, both living and dead. The Rapture and the Resurrection would then prove to be one and the same event. If it's true that the Rapture is the Resurrection, the Church could be here through all of Jacob's trouble side by side with Jacob.

I don't say this to make an already controversial book more controversial. I say it out of a burden for the Church to be prepared for this possibility as many are counting on *not* being here for the real difficulties. I have been concerned for many years that unpreparedness in the troubles of the last days could be one of the causes of the "falling away," a great loss of faith in the Church. Paul warns in 2 Thessalonians 2:14 that a falling away must come before "our gathering together unto Him." That is, those who hope to be raptured well before the last day may lose heart if they must truly endure to the end.

I believe this trust in an early rapture accounts for a lack of interest in the particulars of Romans 11. Much of the Church simply feel they will be in heaven when all of this comes to pass. I've often heard some jokingly call themselves *pan-tribulationists*, who don't want to consider these things, saying it will all "pan out" in the end. I believe the Church and the Jewish people will go through these difficulties together until the last day.

For these reasons, the "fullness of the Gentiles" may not be a reference to the last Gentile being saved before the Rapture of the Church, especially since Israel is to be a light to the nations and bring them life from the dead. If so, how could all the Gentiles who will ever be saved be gone via early rapture? The "fullness of the Gentiles" may mean something else as the Church and Israel may well be in this stormy sea together. The word *fullness* in Romans 11:25 (in the Greek it's *pleroma,* derived from *pleroo*) has as part of its meaning the concept of *fully preaching*. This same word *pleroma* is used a few chapters later by Paul in Romans 15:19 when he says, "I have *fully preached* the gospel of Messiah" (emphasis added). In this light, the "fullness of the Gentiles" being accomplished may mean the fulfilling of the calling of the Gentiles to preach the gospel. This fulfillment does not occur until Israel is provoked to jealousy and takes up her calling.

The fullness is like a pregnancy. God has given the Gentiles the gospel to carry to full term. Israel will then carry it with her. In the very next verse of Romans 11, this fulfillment results in *all of Israel being saved* (see Rom. 11:26). So that when the Gentiles fully preach and provoke the Jewish people to a jealous hunger for their Messiah, and God pours out His Spirit on the Jewish people, the Gentile calling of carrying the gospel alone (without her endtime partner, Israel) comes to a close. And then Israel is aflame, and she and her dear sister, the Church, enter into the time of Jew and Gentile together to close out this age in hot revival amidst tribulation.

Do you see this? Paul is telling the Church not to be unaware of a mystery. A mystery is something heretofore unrevealed: that Jew and Gentile are not only being made one in the Jewish Olive Tree of faith in Jesus—a staggering truth in itself—but that Israel has been partially blinded, so that the Church can have an opportunity to carry the gospel back to Israel. In this way, the Church is to open Israel's eyes *through the mercy* shown to the Church, that "through the mercy shown you they also may obtain mercy" (Rom. 11:31).

The way I read this passage is that the blindness that God has put on Israel is going to be lovingly removed by the Church. And that this is the most important mission of the Church: to restore Israel to her gifts and calling, which are irrevocable in God. It is true that Israel has been blinded to her calling, until now, to carry the gospel to the nations. But, for the sake of God's promises to Abraham and the patriarchs, all the families of the earth will be blessed in their descendants (Gen. 12:3). The Church has been given the awesome task of tending and healing Israel's wounds, of being a nation of Good Samaritans to the nation of Israel, who will once again be beaten and left for dead.

For the parable of the Good Samaritan in Luke 10 was given by Jesus to support the point of a discussion that there is eternal life for those who love God with all their heart and love their neighbor as themselves. In the parable, the religious people (the priest and Levite) first saw a beaten fellow Jew on the road from Jerusalem to Jericho. Whether busy from legitimate appointments or afraid to be beaten themselves by robbers or just lacking compassion, they passed by on the other side of the road, ignoring their countryman stripped of his clothes, wounded, and half dead. We can all identify with failing to risk oneself during someone's time of need. But it was a Samaritan, not even fully Jewish, who crossed the cultural barrier between Jews and Samaritans to exhibit compassion. He stopped his own life to help a Jew. He was no less busy, but he bound up the fallen man's wounds, treated them, and paid his own money to have him further cared for at an inn.

Jesus asks, "Which one was neighbor to him who fell among thieves?"

They answered, "The one who showed mercy on him."

And Jesus replied, "Go and do likewise" (Luke 10:37). There is a truth in the parable beyond the truth that God values deeds of love above cold religion.

I believe the whole true Church is being called upon to go and do likewise: to show mercy to Israel, soon to be fallen among those who would take her inheritance. But it requires a Church who is loving God with all her heart to be such a loving neighbor. That is one reason why such an abundant rain of the Holy Spirit is presently being poured out on the church. And it will be even greater, spawning a revival the likes of which we cannot even imagine!

The church is going to fall so helplessly in love with Jesus because of the grace and mercy poured out on her, that she is going to love Israel into her calling as a light to the nations. And she (Israel) will finally accept her national position of carrying the good news of her Messiah to the nations. As it says, "For if the casting away of them [Israel under partial blindness] is the reconciling of the world [Gentiles called from the nations to carry the gospel] what shall the receiving of them be [Israel awake and carrying her calling of the gospel to the nations] but life from the dead [the whole world ablaze with worldwide revival as a dead world comes alive]" (Rom. 11:15). And all the glory goes to God! "For of Him and through Him and to Him are all things to whom be glory forever. Amen" (Rom. 11:36).

And so chapter 11 of Romans concludes with the mercy of God poured out on both of God's instruments, the Church and Israel, to accomplish the ultimate plan and purpose of God, the endtime worldwide harvest of souls ushering in the Messiah's return. Hallelujah to the all-wise God!

The concepts of Romans 11 do not end with that chapter, however. Romans 12, verses 1 and 2, are part of the same thought. Paul urges the Church, in light of all that's been said in Romans 11:

> I beseech you *therefore*, brethren, by the mercies of God, [mercy to the Gentile and mercy to the Jew] that you present your bodies a living sacrifice, holy, acceptable to God, which is your reasonable service. And do not be conformed to this world, but be transformed by the renewing of your mind, that you may prove what is that good and acceptable and perfect will of God. (Rom. 12:1–2)

He is saying because of these mercies of God, both to the Church and through the Church to Israel, *I beg you* to present your bodies to God as a living, holy sacrifice which is your service to God. He's saying it's going to take an incredible sacrifice on the part of the Church to perform this service to God—in letting God use the Church as a channel of mercy to Israel—but it's good, it's acceptable, and it's the perfect will of God. Yes, there are broader implications in this passage of Romans 12:1–2 of our entire walk with God; but Paul does say "therefore" do this, indicating the prior reasoning of Romans 11. It is a holy sacrifice the church is called to, something only a few have entered into until now. But this sacrifice is prophetic of the final generation, and I believe we will see it fulfilled. It is so holy that Paul says it can only be done by a transformed Church with a renewed mind. Heretofore, the Church has remained too "conformed" to the world's view of Israel and the Jewish people to want to lift Israel's blindness. In the past, when scattered Israel had fallen among thieves, too many passed by on the other side of the road, and too few risked their lives to help. I know that what I'm saying is asking a lot of the Church, but it's not I, but the Lord. When Jewish people are again persecuted in the time of Jacob's trouble, I see the Church as the Good Samaritan to her.

Lord help us to have ears to hear. O the untold riches that belong to those who will believe God and bless Israel in this way.

CHAPTER 5

THE CHURCH: A NATION OF RUTHS

In July 1996 I heard a teaching that presented the Book of Ruth as an allegory about the Church and Israel. This teaching was given by Jonathan Cahn who leads a Messianic congregation named Beth Israel in Garfield, New Jersey. I believe the Lord gave him an insight, which I will share with you. He has been gracious to allow me to share the heart of his teaching in this book, and I thank him for this permission and his ministry and unselfish heart for God.

When I first heard this teaching, I was thrilled because I thought it was true, deep, and important, but I did not think of it again until after I had begun writing this book. The Lord had brought it to my mind, as only He can do in those little "coincidences" that leave us wondering if it was another hint from God or something else. I believe this was God. I had invited a friend, Anthony Voci, to dinner. Anthony is a believing attorney who works with me in my law office. He lives about an hour's drive from the Messianic congregation I attend in Philadelphia where, on Saturday, October 4, 1997, two buses were going to take about sixty of us to be a part of Promise Keepers' "Stand in the Gap" rally in Washington, D.C. More than a million men gathered to praise and worship God and repent for our sins and the sins of America. It was a great event.

Since the buses were leaving at 5:00 A.M. from our congregation's parking lot in Philadelphia, Anthony stayed at our house to get a little more sleep and for the convenience of being a few blocks from the departure site. After dinner and before leaving for Friday evening service at Congregation Beth Yeshua, Anthony was looking through his Bible while I was getting ready for the service.

He had just been reading in the Book of Ruth and asked me what I thought this book was about. I had never studied the Book of Ruth too deeply, but as I began to think for a moment I remembered the heart of Jonathan Cahn's message in the summer of 1996 that the Book of Ruth was an allegory: Ruth, representing the church, loves Naomi, representing Israel, and clings to her. As I was saying this, it hit me that this book of the Bible and Jonathan Cahn's insight were important for what the Lord was trying to get me to understand about Jew and Gentile. And I believe He's given me a further glimpse of this book's application for today. I'm sure more will be understood about this book as events unfold.

Ruth, whose name means "friendship," befriends her mother-in-law, Naomi, in a manner so passionate that this scripture is often used as a wedding vow between loving couples as they express the ideal commitment they hope to have for each other. Ruth said to Naomi,

Entreat me not to leave you, or to turn back from following after you; for wherever you go, I will go; and
wherever you lodge, I will lodge; your people shall be
my people, and your God, my God. Where you die, I
will die, and there will I be buried. The Lord do so to
me, and more also, if anything but death parts you and
me. (Ruth 1:16–17)

Ruth is pledging her life to Naomi. She says, in effect,
"If I leave you except for any reason but death, may God
abandon me and worse!" And she says she will die where
Naomi dies, giving of her strength to sustain Naomi. Can
you imagine selflessly committing your goals and life purposes so thoroughly? It reminds me of Jesus' statement,
"Greater love hath no man than this, to lay down his life
for his friends" (John 15:13). Ruth was laying down all hope
of eternal life except through clinging to Naomi.

The context of this vow of Ruth is that Naomi (Israel),
whose name means "my pleasantness," and her husband,
Elimelech, which means "my God is king," leave Bethlehem
for neighboring Moab because of a famine in Israel. They
escape the scarcity of food in Israel but not God's judgment
as they live in the scarcity of God's presence in exile in hea-
then Moab. They take their two sons; Mahlon, which means
"sick," and Chilion, which means "pining away." Their
names give us a good picture of Jewish exile from the rich
spiritual blessings God is longing to pour out on His ancient people. Mahlon marries the Gentile Ruth, and Chilion
marries the Gentile Orpah. During this family's ten-year
stay in Moab, Elimelech, Mahlon, and Chilion all die, leaving widows respectively in Naomi, Ruth and Orpah.

The family left Bethlehem, which in Hebrew means
"House of Bread." It is the place of Jesus' birth, the One

Who is also the Bread of Life. In effect, we see Naomi (Israel) reject the calling of carrying the gospel (the Bread of Life) and go into exile for it. It speaks of the dispersion from their land, which Israel has experienced for the last 1900 years.

In this prophetic book, national Israel (Naomi), in rejecting the Messiah's gospel, has lost all her sense that "my God is king" (Elimelech dies). She is bereaved of her sons as well. But when she hears that the Lord is visiting His people in the homeland by giving them bread, Naomi desires to return. (Ruth 1:6) Salvation of the Jewish people has begun; God's blessing again being poured out in Israel signals the end of exile. The Jewish people will soon desire to return to Israel, when their reputation vanishes after Israel destroys Damascus and they are persecuted, and when the Spirit of God is again poured out in Israel.

The Book of Ruth has much to say to us today. The land of Israel was restored in 1948. Bread of salvation is once again being given to the Jewish people; God is raising up Jews who believe in their Messiah *Yeshua* (Jesus). Millions of exiled Jewish people have returned from many nations, and more are returning from Russia and soon from all nations because it's time for the great harvest. God is regathering His people in these last days from their long scattering in all the nations so He can pour out on them the Spirit of His Son, the Bread of Life.

Naomi's daughters-in-law, Ruth and Orpah, both begin the journey to return to Israel with Naomi, but Naomi urges them to find their life's fulfillment with their own people and the gods of Moab. Naomi wants her daughters-in-law to be happy, but she cannot imagine what joy could be theirs in unity with her. She has no spiritual vision beyond a sense that she must return to her homeland. Possibly she is even rejecting them, refusing their company. I believe Orpah ("stiff neck") and Ruth ("friend") together make up the two parts of the Church. Orpah, who yields to Naomi's suggestion, returns home to Moab and represents those believers who have no real heart-burden for the Jewish people. The Orpah segment of the Church identifies more with the unsaved nations than with Israel. She does not have the grace to yield herself to God's plan for Naomi (Israel). She does not discern the spiritual significance of clinging to Israel, because she's blinded to this deep thing of God.

Ruth, on the other hand, will not listen to Naomi. Her love is so strong for Naomi that wild horses, and even Naomi's rejection, couldn't pull her away. Why? She has been given grace from the Lord to resist what is natural and worldly. It is so easy in the world not to identify with the Jew. Almost the entire world is doing it. These days UN votes on issues concerning Israel are usually landslides against her. It's hard to believe that just fifty years ago the UN voted for Israel to be a sovereign nation, formed in a single day as Isaiah prophesied (see Isa. 66:8). One recent UN vote as to what to do to Israel for building a settlement of homes in her own capital of Jerusalem resulted in a vote of 172 in favor of sanctioning Israel, with only three against sanctioning Israel. The United States, Israel, and Micronesia were the only dissenting nations among six billion people on our planet criticizing Israel. Where is Micronesia anyway? I wonder how she's going to be blessed.

But Ruth had a burning zeal that could only come from God. She represents that portion of the Church who has what we Jewish believers call in Gentile believers "a Jewish heart." Even more so, she is able, like the apostle Paul and

Moses, to wish herself accursed if Israel would only be saved. And she's not even Jewish as they were!

This is clearly a supernatural love, and that's why I'm writing this book. I believe God is pouring out this type of supernatural love on the Church today, and I'm writing to expound on it and encourage it. I have been a believer for approximately twenty-three years now, and I've not seen or heard of anything like what has been going on in the last few years in the Church. I have been in worship meetings organized by various Christian groups and heard of many others where spontaneously, without plan or agenda, Israel or Messianic Jews or something about Jewishness bursts forth onto the meeting. I have seen, rising among those in the Church, a new and fresh love for Jewish things: love for the Jewish roots of our common faith in Jesus, for the Jewish festivals, and for Israel. Many of my Messianic Jewish friends and I have been scratching our heads wondering what is going on. For the last twenty-five years or so the Messianic movement has begun to see independent Messianic congregations increase from only a handful to hundreds worldwide. But there has been precious little affirmation from the Church for our movement. Yes, there have been individuals and churches here and there with a deep love for Jewish people and Israel and Messianic Jews, but not on the scale that is presently taking place. It seems that the more God pours out His Spirit in this latter-rain revival, the more He pours out within this revival a love for Israel and the Jewish people.

Is God raising up in the Church a Ruth generation? I believe so. I believe this is the true calling of the Church, to reveal the Messiah and His great love to unbelieving Israel so she can, in turn, be a light back to the nations.

Upon Naomi's return to Israel she tells her friends not to call her Naomi ("my pleasantness"), but to call her Mara ("bitterness"), because the Lord has dealt bitterly with her in exile (Ruth 1:20). God uses *Ruth* to restore Naomi to be God's pleasantness in a mutually loving relationship. And so the Church and Israel together will show the world the love they have for one another. The world will be able to see modeled in this special love that the prejudices and hatred that separates nations and ethnic groups are wrong. The world will see in this unlikely love affair that God is pouring out love on the Church and Israel, the two folds of His flock. And the world will respond with revival! Ruth's act of love for Naomi is nothing less than an expression of her love for Naomi's God, Who has given her so much grace.

As we continue through the Book of Ruth we see that Ruth and Naomi come back to Bethlehem "in the beginning of the barley harvest" (Ruth 1:22). Barley was the lowliest of the grains. Barley was poor-man's bread. This harvest represents Messiah's harvest of the lowly and humble of heart, and represents our generation in which Israel has been restored at the time of the great endtime harvest. To make ends meet, Ruth begins to beg for barley for herself and Naomi in the field of a rich and mighty and spiritual man named Boaz. This represents the true Church interceding on behalf of Israel—that God would save her, giving her the precious bread of life.

Boaz's name means "in Him is strength." He is a close relative of Naomi and is a type of the Messiah Jesus. Boaz notices Ruth gleaning in his fields and finds out she is Naomi's Gentile daughter-in-law who has been good to Naomi. So he tells her she should glean (or pick up food) for herself and Naomi from his field and not from another. He gives her protection and heaps favors upon her to glean

63

among the sheaves and not the fallen pieces, and to eat and drink with his harvesters. Naturally Ruth asks Boaz, "Why have I found grace in your eyes that you should take knowledge of me, seeing I am a stranger?" (Ruth 2:10). Boaz answers her:

> It has been fully reported to me, all that you have done for your mother-in-law since the death of your husband, and how you have left your father and your mother and the land of your birth, and have come to a people whom you did not know before. The Lord repay your work, and a full reward be given you by the Lord God of Israel, under Whose wings you have come for refuge. (Ruth 2:11–12)

Because Ruth (the Church) adopted Naomi (Israel) and her people, Boaz (Jesus) bestows abundant blessings on Ruth. Her love and intercession are greatly rewarded.

When Ruth returns that evening to Naomi and shows her all of the grain she has received from Boaz and the favor he has shown her, they agree that Ruth should stay with Boaz until the end of the harvest. Therefore, because of Naomi, Ruth is directed into a blessing from the God of Israel. Israel has provided the world with the Messiah, though she herself has not yet found Him. It is so interesting that Naomi does not simply go to Boaz directly, now that Naomi is again living in his town, but Naomi's only contact with Boaz (Jesus) comes through Ruth. This demonstrates that Israel's blindness to Jesus is destined to be removed by the Church through prayer and deeds.

Naomi counsels Ruth to seek Boaz as a husband under the Levirate law of the *kinsman redeemer*, where the nearest relative could redeem a widow's heritage by marrying the widow to raise up children and a name for the deceased relative's husband. In this case, the lands of Elimelech, Naomi's deceased husband, could be redeemed; and Ruth, the wife of Mahlon, Naomi's son, could be married. Boaz agrees and marries Ruth, and she bears him a son named Obed, which means "servant," "service," or even "worship." Obed is the blessing to Ruth from Boaz. Yet when the women in Israel hear of Obed's birth, they rejoice and say to Naomi:

> Blessed be the Lord, Who has not left you this day without a close relative [Boaz who represents Jesus]; and may his name be famous in Israel! And may he be to you a restorer of life and a nourisher of your old age; for your daughter-in-law, who loves you, who is better to you than seven sons, has borne him. (Ruth 4:14–15)

So the relationship of Boaz (Jesus) and Ruth (the Church) produces an offspring of service to God that becomes the continuation of Naomi's very name, family line, and heritage in Abraham's covenant—which was in jeopardy of being extinguished for lack of an heir. The child Obed—symbolically, service to God, borne by Ruth—restores the lineage of Naomi (Israel) who has literally come to life. Naomi has her calling restored. Ruth is better to Naomi than what seven sons could produce in heirs for her, for Ruth has given Naomi a reintroduction through Obed to Boaz (Jesus). Salvation comes to Naomi (Israel) through the seed (Obed) of the calling of service to God and grace of Boaz (Jesus) given to and through Ruth (the Church).

And now for the best part:

And Naomi took the child and laid it in her bosom and *became nurse unto it*. And Naomi's neighbors gave the child a name, saying, There is a son born to Naomi, and they called his name Obed. (Ruth 4:16–17; emphasis added)

God is supernaturally grafting Israel back into her calling through Ruth's love. And all Israel approves.

Naomi became nurse to Boaz and Ruth's child! The neighbors even say the child is born to her. Hallelujah! God is awesome! Through the Church, Israel is saved and has God as her husband again. The service of the Church to Naomi, through God's grace, even allows Naomi to become *nurse* to Obed. Naomi, an aging woman who was too old to glean with Ruth in Boaz's fields, surely without milk in her breasts (having only two grown sons long deceased), is miraculously able to nurse a child. Obed is not nursed to health from sickness, but wet-nursed by Naomi, who has become as vibrant as if she herself had given birth to Obed. And the other women even say, "a son is born to Naomi."

Are you getting this? This is a prophetic picture of the Church and Israel supernaturally married to Jesus, together supernaturally giving service to God, and fulfilling their callings and destinies. The Church will perform its role (which we discussed from Romans 11) of calling Israel back to faith by intensely loving her. The fullness, or pregnancy, of the gospel of the Gentiles has come in, and Israel is being saved by it (Rom. 11:25–26).

I believe Obed represents the gospel of Jesus. Through Naomi and her relationship to God, Ruth has met Boaz (Jesus). Through Naomi's counsel (the Word of God through the Jewish people), Ruth has received salvation from Boaz and the precious gospel to preach (Obed).

The Church has carried the gospel for many centuries now just as Ruth carried Obed in her womb. He grew and developed there, and now, after these many years, the Church will lay the calling of carrying the gospel onto the breasts of Israel. The gospel still needs something from Naomi's heritage. In large measure the gospel will be empowered *because* Ruth has had the grace to honor Naomi. Without the Church reaching that incredible place in God, Naomi could not be stirred to a *miraculous* expression of love for Obed. This child—the fullness of the Gentiles and the grace from Boaz—represents a living testimony of how wonderful Jesus is. But now that Naomi (Israel) has again become God's pleasantness, she is squarely carrying and advancing (nursing) the Kingdom of Jesus with her own grace because God has commanded a blessing on her at the place of unity with Ruth (the Church).

We may wonder why there's no mention of Ruth nursing Obed. The implication is clear that Ruth is well able to do so, but her love for Naomi has led her to take a step back in her own baby's (the gospel's) development. I believe Naomi coming to the foreground in the gospel's life certainly does not mean that Ruth is excluded, but has voluntarily chosen to be in and among the restored Israel. God's calling for Israel must be recognized by the Church before Israel will recognize it. The Church must give Israel the idea or revelation through an intense intercession and supernatural love. I can see Ruth even asking herself, "Why am I laying my child on Naomi like this?" all the while knowing it was right to do, because it was God's prophetic urging to Ruth contained within the great love He had given Ruth for Naomi.

I see the Church selflessly desiring and urging Israel (possibly at first the Messianic Jewish movement as the remnant of Israel) to take the lead in Obed's life (the gospel). And miracles will flow as they did among the apostles in the Book of Acts. And then all Israel will be enflamed with the gospel and take it as a torch into the nations. They will bring life from the dead as a messenger heralding the coming of her King Messiah, as a corporate John the Baptist for Jesus' first coming and as a corporate Elijah to herald Jesus' second coming. They will announce His coming and prepare the people for it.

Though Ruth has sacrificed to help Naomi, Ruth has not been diminished by it. Instead, she has pleased Boaz by loving Naomi. Boaz shall surely pour out even more grace on Ruth. Likewise, the Church shall be greatly rewarded by God for loving Israel into God's kingdom and her calling.

I can't say I see the form that this will take or the interplay between the saved and unsaved Jewish people or the government of Israel. But I believe the gospel will become Jewish again, and the Church will not be jealous but excited about it!

CHAPTER 6

THE CHURCH TODAY

I t is now time for the endtime harvest. The world is in the midst of the greatest revival since Pentecost. In fact, it's already greater. Many more people have been saved in this century than in any other; possibly more already than all previous centuries combined. Some say there have been more martyrs in the Church as well. Korea has been in revival for the last twenty years, as has Argentina and much of South America. In China, 100 million believers have been saved in the last ten years and are meeting secretly in house churches. Scores of other places are experiencing unprecedented outpourings of the Holy Spirit. We can barely keep track of all that God is doing in these last days, and this is only the beginning. Israel has been restored as a nation and one-third of world Jewry has returned to their homeland. An indigenous body of Messianic Jews is in place in Israel and elsewhere and growing marvelously. A single event such as war or economic collapse is capable of producing worldwide persecution of Jews at any moment. The Jew has been blamed as a scapegoat in the past, and something as serious as an unconventional destruction of Damascus as described in Isaiah 17 could send Jewish people into hiding from the serious persecution likely to erupt.

Does it sound farfetched to you? It does to me. If it hadn't happened countless times in history, I'd say it's impossible. But it's not impossible. Persecution and an intense Holy Spirit outpouring may be the only way the Church and Israel will be brought together into their glorious joint destiny as the people of God truly becoming One New Man, "that He might reconcile them both [Jew and Gentile] unto God in one body through the cross, thereby putting to death the enmity [the hatred between these two groups]" (Eph. 2:16).

Jew and Gentile comprise a single spiritual body existing invisibly in Jesus, a spiritual Olive Tree. It is built upon the foundation of the Jewish apostles and prophets with Jesus as the chief cornerstone (Eph. 2:20). It is a spiritual building that *builds itself up* in love (Eph. 4:16). Love (God) builds it. No outsider can build this house of a joint Jewish-Gentile kingdom in Jesus. It is built by supernatural love on the order of Ruth and Naomi, through the grace of Boaz (Jesus). It remains unbuilt when we are estranged from one another and even look the other way at each other's calamity.

The coming calamity of the Jewish people's worldwide persecution is going to present the Church with an opportunity to build this house by supernatural love, a love we've not witnessed since Acts 2, when the followers of Jesus held all things in common for each other. Will the church look on Israel's affliction with the compassion of a Ruth or with the deedless affection or indifference of an Orpah? As with the story of the Good Samaritan, will the Church cross over to the other side of the street in religious "business as usual" when she sees Israel beaten by heritage-robbers and laying half-dead in a ditch? Or will the Church risk her own safety and lay down her own programs to bind Israel's wounds and participate in a miraculous explosion of the gospel in and through Israel?

I know full well there are many good reasons that the Church has not loved Israel in this way. I do not judge the Church for not taking up this calling. Please hear my heart. Israel has similarly not taken up her calling to be the kind of light to the nations she is called to be. I do not judge Israel, either. She has good reasons for fearing the Church. I am not writing to fix any blame whatsoever. If it sounds that way, it is not intended. I am writing to make the Church hungry for the kind of blessings Ruth obtained. I am asking the church to pray for the grace necessary to do this. I know how easy it is to sit by while another person's need is placed squarely before me. I am no different, I am no better.

As an example, on the bus ride back to Philadelphia from the "Stand in the Gap" million-man rally in Washington, D.C., on October 4, 1997, one of the men who went with us could not find our bus in the myriad of buses parked at RFK Stadium. We were told to be at the bus by 6:00 P.M. for the return ride. It was not emphasized that the bus would promptly leave, but at 6:08 the bus company we had hired said, "We're leaving now."

I was disturbed that one of our brothers would be stranded on a Saturday night in Washington and have to find his way back to Philadelphia alone. I stood up and yelled out something like, "Wait! That's not right. We can't just leave this guy!" Immediately the female bus driver shot back, "Well, if you don't like it, you can get off now, too!" And you know what? That upset me. But I didn't say another word. I sat down and quietly rode home with thirty other quiet men on our bus. I was upset with myself, but it showed me just how easy it is to do nothing in the face of another's need.

This is on a smaller scale than the calling of the Church or Israel, but this is our soulish human nature of self-preservation. Without grace from God I don't believe the Church can lay down her life for Israel. Without the grace of God Israel would not lay down her life for the Church either.

But Jesus has come to give us that grace. He has come to give us power to be like Him. He is a giver, and He gives us the Holy Spirit freely. It's amazing that such a treasure as the very Spirit of God would live in us. He gave *Himself* away for the joy of building this Jewish-Gentile eternal family, that we would partake of His divine nature, His sinless flesh, His cleansing blood, and dwell with Him forever.

This kind of grace is being poured out now. We cannot judge these present times by the past. This is going to happen suddenly as other great events of the Bible. There was no way to look at them with the natural eye to see them coming. The opening of the Red Sea, the birth of Jesus, and the outpouring of Pentecost all came suddenly. Don't fall into the trap of preparing for tomorrow based only upon the needs of today. Don't be like the scoffers in the world who will say in the last days, "Where is the promise of His coming? For since the fathers fell asleep all things continue as they were from the beginning of the creation" (2 Pet. 3:4). Many things are going to change before Jesus returns, and we are going to live through times that we have never seen before. Everything is going to change, even the nature of the faith.

CHAPTER 7

PARADIGM SHIFT IN THE OLIVE TREE?

Jesus said He only did what He saw His Father doing (John 5:19). And that's really all our job is as believers: to see what God is doing and do it. I believe the Church will go on to lay herself down for Israel, to add Israel to the Body of Messiah, because I believe God has decided to do this in and through the Church. And when she sees the Father is doing this, she will do it.

But though I believe the Ruth portion of the Church will be excited to present Obed (the gospel) unto Israel to carry, there may also be a practical reason for doing so. God may have the Church prefer Israel in carrying the gospel because she herself is going to be persecuted. Israel may be added to the Body of Messiah at this strategic time through the mercy of a Church who will soon be in need of mercy. Even as I write this, I sense a certain sadness that the Ruth portion of the Church will suffer greatly in her standing up for the Jewish people. I am reminded of Corrie ten Boom and her family, who as Dutch Christians chose to hide Jews during World War II, knowing full well if they were caught they would be killed. Corrie and her sister did go into the concentration camp where her sister was tortured and died, but Corrie was miraculously preserved. Corrie's name is enshrined in honor at Israel's Holocaust museum, *Yad Vashem*, in Jerusalem.

It may be that we will see the Church also lose the favor and protection of the many national governments that she presently enjoys. The Muslim and Communist nations have already long ago withdrawn cover for the Church in their nations. The Church in the West may suffer the same when one-world government pressures mount and believers in Jesus become more of an offense to the all-ways-to-God-are-equal mantra. The Church could become an underground movement, as it is in China today, with 100 million Chinese believers worshiping Jesus in house churches, hiding from the Communist government. The same is true throughout Southeast Asia and Cuba.

Maybe Ruth will move to the background in Obed's (the gospel's) life because the public platform of favor from governments to proclaim the gospel is removed and only in Israel will there be an ability to share the gospel openly.

The present controversial bill, recently proposed in Israel's legislature, to make preaching the gospel a crime in Israel upon penalty of one year in prison may have surfaced at this time as an attempt by the devil to choke off Israel's ability to receive the gospel. I believe God will defeat this measure one way or another; but if not, the gospel is going to catch fire in Israel anyway, as prophesied (see

Zech. 12:10). Nonetheless, the Church may join herself to Israel as the gospel explodes there miraculously.

There is a scripture well known among Messianic Jews but unfamiliar in most Christian circles. Zechariah 8:23 reads: "Thus says the Lord of hosts: In those days ten men from every language of the nations shall grasp the sleeve of a Jewish man, saying, 'Let us go with you, for we have heard that God is with you.'" This seems to indicate that Jewish people are returning to Israel and ten times the number of Christians are returning with them.

I am hopeful that in God's regathering of the Jewish people to Israel, there will be many among the Ruth portion of the Church who literally return to physical Israel with returning Naomi. If ten times the amount of Jewish people grab hold of Jewish shirts on their way back to their homeland in Israel, there could be a sizeable remnant of Ruths among us. If, for example, five million Jews return, that could mean 50 million Christians with them. Where would Israel put them? The land God promised to Abraham in Genesis 15:18—from the Nile River to the Euphrates River—is more than adequate. And Israel was instructed in the Torah to receive without discrimination those from the nations who desired to sojourn with her (see Exod. 12:48–49).

The church being driven underground in the near future could be part of a paradigm shift in the model of faith in Jesus. If the Church is persecuted while the gospel explodes in Israel, this may be the only above-ground, visible expression of the faith, and it would once again be a Jewish expression with the Church a part of it.

In the beginning of Jesus' ministry, faith in Him was almost exclusively a Jewish commodity. This merely continued the status quo of faith in God being Jewish, as Jesus went only to the house of Israel. Prior to the time when Gentiles began believing in Jesus, the Gentiles were idol worshipers in the nations. So before Jesus' ministry, the only way a Gentile could have a relationship with the true God was to become a Jew.

The Book of Acts is a record of Jewish preachers going to Jewish listeners until Acts chapter 8 when Philip preaches to Samaritans, and then in Acts chapter 10 where Peter preaches to the Roman centurion Cornelius and his household. Peter needed a supernatural vision to encourage him to go to the Gentile home of Cornelius. The Jewish believers at that time were amazed that Gentiles had a part in this faith through *their* Messiah, but in time, Jewish believers came to be engulfed by a sea of Gentile believers, which came to be known as the Church.

When Israel was scattered into all nations in A.D. 70 by the Romans, the Jewish believers began to lose their visible expression of faith in *Yeshua* (Jesus). Jewish believers through the centuries were encouraged, often pressured or even threatened, to abandon their heritage as believing Jews and become Christians, expressing their faith in and among the Church's visible structure. This still takes place today to some extent.

I believe this was made possible because national Israel had lost their homeland and, as a people, had no visible public platform on which to stand. We were dispersed among the nations for more than 1900 years. Living in foreign lands, Jewish believers adopted a foreign expression of their faith. However, when Israel became a nation again in 1948, her national platform was restored. In 1967 her worship center of Jerusalem was returned to her, and now a Jewish expression of faith in the Messiah is possible and has begun to be raised up in the form of hundreds of Messianic congregations worldwide. Messianic Jews are seeking to recover a Jewish expression of faith in their Jewish Messiah, Yeshua (Jesus). Biblical festivals are celebrated; the original sixth day Sabbath is often observed and ancient Jewish culture and thinking is incorporated in various ways into the worship and study of the scriptures. Many of these congregations are in Israel and are exclusively Hebrew speaking. Those outside Israel have a mixture of Hebrew and English worship or whatever language is spoken locally. The point is that there is a nation in Israel again, and the faith has the potential, for the first time in almost two thousand years, of becoming Jewish again. If persecution does break out against Jews in the nations, there is now a Jewish homeland to flee to. Ironically, the Church has no such haven, but if the church becomes persecuted along with Jews, it would be the first time that a national Israel would be in existence as a haven for both Christians and Jews. Of course, the Church already is persecuted, but if there were a simultaneous worldwide persecution of both groups, Christians may indeed join themselves to Jewish people returning to Israel as Zechariah 8 prophesies.

This could present a shift in the model of the faith, as a greater and greater percentage of Jewish people continue to accept Jesus as their Messiah and Lord. What has long been Israel (Jewish believers) in and among the Church presenting the gospel to the nations, could well become the Church in and among Israel presenting the gospel to the nations. In the metaphor of the Olive Tree of Romans 11, the Jewish branches are to be grafted back into their *own* Olive Tree (Rom. 11:24), bringing life from the dead to the nations. Ruth celebrates Israel's harvest as a *Jewess* married to Boaz, radiating with love as she and Naomi together glorify what Boaz has done. The Body of Messiah adds its Jewish branches and is restored to its Jewish character, prepared to receive unto itself the rest of the Gentiles called out from every nation.

Could this be why the Church is now hungering after her Jewish roots, celebrating Passover and the festivals, drawing new meaning into her worship from Israel's heritage? She certainly should. It's the Church's heritage too. Jesus has died to give it to her. The blessings of Abraham have surely come upon her, but is the Church willing to become as a Jewess? This is the mystery of the will of God Paul spoke of, hidden from the ages:

> That in the dispensation of the fullness of times He might gather together in one all things in Messiah both which are in Heaven and which are on Earth; even in Him. In whom also we have obtained an inheritance, being predestined according to the purpose of Him Who works all things after the counsel of His own will; that we should be to the praise of His glory, who first trusted [Israel] in whom you [Gentiles] also trusted after you heard the Word of Truth, the gospel of your salvation. (Eph. 1:10–12)

Paul explains the mystery of Messiah: "That the Gentiles should be fellow heirs and of the same body and partakers of His promise in Messiah by the gospel" (Eph. 3:6).

Though God may be restoring this model or paradigm of faith to its Jewish origin, it is not to exalt its Jewishness over the Church. Paul writes, "And [have] put on the new man who is renewed in knowledge according to the image of Him Who created him, where there is neither Greek nor Jew, circumcised nor uncircumcised, barbarian, Scythian, slave nor free, but Messiah is all and in all" (Col. 3:10–11). God definitely chose to create the Jewish nation, but He has made it undesirable, a measuring rod for the humble. In this way, the thoroughly humble can be received into the kingdom of a Jewish Messiah, but the proud who refuse such a lowly thing are excluded. For our Messiah has not come to this world in grandeur, but was born in a stable among animals and stench. It is the wisdom of God to reserve eternal life in undesirable places for the desperately hungry.

Church, come and be undesirable with Israel so we can preach the gospel together to the desperately hungry of the nations. Will you love Israel to life at the expense of your glory? For the glory of your God? Israel's God?

Will you let the paradigm of faith shift back to being a Jewish faith again? Would you help the paradigm shift if you believed it was God's plan? I believe so.

CHAPTER 8

ISAIAH 58 IS PROPHETIC

W hy does God want the Church to bless and even lay down her life for Israel and the Jewish people? Because He loves the Church and wants to bless her. God has already given anyone with ears to hear a fantastic principle of blessing or cursing Abraham's seed. The wise will see this as a great opportunity to be pleasing to God and to be blessed by Him. The foolish will see it as foolishness, as with any other plan and purpose of God.

But clearly God is looking for ways to bless us. His eye is upon us for blessing, and His hand is upon us for good. It's going to be more than a little embarrassing for those who missed out on blessing the Jewish people. But let's look at Isaiah 58 together, where I believe God is giving the Church a blueprint for blessing Israel.

Not long ago I woke up from a night's sleep with an overpowering thought: "Isaiah 58 is prophetic." When I awoke, I remembered having had this thought in my sleep several times that night, and it was the first thought on my mind in the morning. And it wouldn't go away until I searched it out and meditated upon it. I reasoned, "Well, Isaiah 58 *is* among the final chapters of the Book of Isaiah, which are also prophetic." But then it came to me: the Church is going to live out Isaiah 58 toward Israel in the Church's process of becoming a bride to Jesus, "without spot or wrinkle or any such thing" (Eph. 5:27).

"Cry aloud, spare not, lift up thy voice like a trumpet, and show My people their transgression, and the house of Jacob their sins" (Isa. 58:1).

This is prophetic because the Church is going to show Israel her sins by the Church's loving example to Israel in her time of trouble. This will be a prophetic act of demonstration by the Church of what Israel is to be to the nations. The Church will be to Israel a model of the selfless light of love and compassion that Israel was called to be and has refused. To date, the Church has refused as well. However, Israel will see that rejecting Jesus was a sin; that she is called to preach Him and His ways to the nations.

God says in Isaiah 58 that Israel has only been fasting according to long-held traditions, but not for the purposes that God has chosen, namely: (1) to deal her bread to the hungry, (2) to bring the poor that are cast out to her house, (3) to cover the naked, and (4) to refrain from hiding her eyes from her own flesh in need (Isa. 58:7, paraphrased). These are the deeds of the true believer. These are the very things that God is interested in finding in our lives. These are the very things the Church will do for Israel during Jacob's time of trouble. And it will be a powerful object lesson.

Matthew 25:31–46 is a picture of the judgment of the nations. There the sheep are separated from the goats based on having shown mercy to one of the least of Jesus' brethren. Look how the mercy there takes the same form as the deeds done in Isaiah 58. Jesus says to the righteous,

> For I was *hungry* and you gave me meat; I was thirsty and you gave me drink. I was a stranger and you *took me in*, *naked* and you clothed me. I was sick and you visited me. I was in prison and you came to me. . . . Inasmuch as you did it to the least of these My brethren, you have done it unto Me. (Matt. 25:35–36, 40)

Many believe Jesus is referring to the Jewish people as "His brethren." Jesus says: As you did to them, you did to Me. And He told the Samaritan woman at the well that "salvation is of the Jew" (John 4:22). Can it be that Jesus so identifies with the Jewish people that the nations are blessed with eternal life or cursed with eternal punishment based on their treatment of the Jew? For some Gentiles, their only contact with a Jew is Jesus, and they'll be judged by how they treat him. For those who meet and mistreat Jews and refuse to bless them, how can it be said they love the King of the Jews, Jesus?

When the Church sees the Jewish people in the throes of a world gone mad with persecution fever, I believe a significant portion of the Church (the Ruth portion) will have the grace from God to feed, clothe, and offer safety to Jewish people attempting to flee from the nations to the safety of the land of Israel. The grace to do this selfless and risky act of blessing Jewish people is already being poured out on much of the Church . Many Christians who are experiencing a love for Israel will find the heroic courage to help Jews on the way to their homeland in Israel.

As it implies in Isaiah 58:8, those Christians who break free from the selfishness of "normal living" into this type of loving your neighbor as yourself, their "light shall break forth as the morning" and their "health shall spring forth speedily." Their righteousness shall go before them and "the glory of the Lord shall be [their] rear guard."

Truly this is the Church Jesus is coming back for. This is the Church without spot or wrinkle or any such thing. This is a people who won't just wish the Jewish people well by saying "be warmed and filled" but fail to tangibly give that which is needed, as James 2:15 warns. But their faith will be expressed by their *deeds* of love. It is this Spirit of giving that will bring revival to the Church as she has never known. It is intimacy with her God that is the church's reward, even the glory of the Lord!

Many times we cry out to the Lord that we want more of Him in our lives, but we don't realize that He and His presence are manifested to us when we *act* on loving our neighbor as ourselves. We ask for greater intimacy with God, but when He sends people into our lives who present opportunities to give of ourselves and our wealth, we refuse. It seems to us that the prayer for intimacy is not being answered, but God is answering by sending us needy people. This prayer is going to be answered for the Church in the form of the Jewish people. God is going to present the Church with one last chance, a final opportunity to have His glory without measure.

> Then you shall call, and the Lord will answer; You shall cry, and He will say, "Here I am." If you take away the yoke from your midst, the pointing of the finger, and speaking wickedness, if you extend your soul to the hungry, and satisfy the afflicted soul, then your light shall dawn in the darkness, and your darkness shall be as the noonday. The Lord will guide you continually, and sat-

isfy your soul in drought, and strengthen your bones; you shall be like a watered garden, and like a spring of water, whose waters do not fail. (Isa. 58:9–11)

And so Isaiah 58 is truly prophetic. It is the very calling of the Church in action, to provoke Israel to jealousy by showing mercy, for God has chosen the Church as His vessel to model mercy to the Jewish people. The pointing of the finger (in Isaiah 58) refers to criticism. Much of the Church has criticized the Jewish people. This needs to be put away for the Church's light to break forth. "When the poor and needy seek water and there is none, and their tongue fails for thirst, I the Lord will hear them; I the God of Israel will not forsake them" (Isa. 41:17). God says He's going to help the poor and needy, and God could do it directly; but He wants the Church to have the blessing of doing it.

This reminds me of when I was a young boy of six or seven years. My father would take me with him in his business to collect money from his customers for goods he had sold them. We would drive from customer to customer in my dad's car. When we would enter the customer's house, my dad would announce "I have my helper with me today." It always brought a smile to the customer's face as we all realized that I was a small boy and wasn't really helping my dad to accomplish something that he couldn't have done on his own. But he allowed me to receive the customer's money and hand it to him. He could have done it himself directly, but he wanted to honor me. He wanted me to have the experience of doing a grown-up thing.

In the same way, God wants the Church to do godly things. He wants the Church to enjoy for eternity the reward of spending herself for the Jewish people He loves, a people who are considered vile by so much of the world. Though God could do it Himself supernaturally, He wants the Church to experience what it means to be like Jesus— Who, while we were still enemies of God, poured Himself out in an agonizing death, taking upon Himself every sin, every sickness, every perversion, every burden of all of humanity for the sheer joy of enabling us to fulfill our God-given destinies. The Church is helping Israel fulfill her destiny and is going to be like God, a godly bride, fit for His Son. Hallelujah! Glory to our wonderful Lord.

The barriers of pride that separate denominations, nationalities, ethnic groups, tribes, and tongues, as well as Gentile and Jew, are yokes of bondage from the enemy of our souls. These are not from God. God says the fast *He* has chosen is to break these yokes and to set the oppressed free (Isa. 58:6). The Church is rapidly approaching the day when she will be faced with ugly persecution of both Jewish people and herself and she will act to break these yokes of bondage in prophetic fulfillment and symbolic example to Israel. When Jewish people see this, they will know *Yeshua* (Jesus) is their Messiah.

As Jesus prayed in John 17:20–23, the oneness of the Church and Israel will release the power of God with a force that will ignite the nations in revival. And the oppressed and weary will be set free. As Zechariah prophesies:

> And I will pour out on the house of David and on the inhabitants of Jerusalem the Spirit of grace and supplication; then they will look on Me whom they pierced. Yes, they will mourn for Him as one mourns for his only son, and grieve for Him as one grieves for a firstborn. . . . In that day a fountain shall be opened for the house of

David and for the inhabitants of Jerusalem, for sin and for uncleanness. (Zech. 12:10, 13:1)

Our God is an awesome God. He has ordained the Church to be the instrument of such outpouring on Israel. It truly is a privilege to worship and obey Him.

CHAPTER 9

GLORY IS SHIFTING: FROM THE NATIONS TO JERUSALEM

In preparation for the paradigm shift in the Olive Tree of faith in Jesus from a Gentile framework to a Jewish framework, the glory of God is going to shift from the nations to the nation of Israel.

I have heard several prophetic words in the last few years from prominent Christian leaders to the effect that they have seen in the Spirit an archway of light or glory shooting from Philadelphia to Jerusalem, somehow connecting these cities. Some of these leaders have come to Philadelphia and actually related to us, in citywide worship meetings there, that they saw this arch in their spirit. I believe that there is indeed an important connection in the Spirit between these two important cities.

It is no secret that for most of the twentieth century the main proponent of the gospel worldwide has been America, the nation founded on the desire to worship God in freedom. America even mirrors the Church in being a nation of people called out from every nation. And America has received refugees from every place to the land of the free. It is fair to say that in the realm of the Spirit, America has been the head of the nations and the seat of God's glory among the nations.

Without getting mired in the point, I believe there was a time when Great Britain was similarly that head of the nations, and she passed this mantle to America over the course of several centuries. Finally, in the twentieth century, Great Britain, still operating in her anointed position as head of the nations, first proposed then opposed the land grant in Palestine to the Jewish people for their restored national homeland of Israel. Great Britain bowed to the pressure of the Arab nations, who bitterly opposed the Balfour Declaration of 1917. This reversal by England delayed until 1948 the formation of the Jewish state. When the holocaust of Europe ensued, there was no homeland to which persecuted Jews could flee. No doubt this increased the souls lost in the Holocaust. The land was being administered under the British mandate. And it is well documented that many boats full of Jews escaping from Nazi occupation and certain death in Europe were sent back by the British. These Jewish people eventually perished in concentration camps because the British feared Arab displeasure over increasing Jewish immigration in Palestine. I believe this was Britain's missed opportunity for tremendous blessing. Soon after this her leadership as an empire upon which the "sun never sets" as well as her position as chief steward of the glory of the gospel of Jesus was lost.

The powerful covenant from God Almighty in the principle of blessing or cursing Abraham's seed operated against

Great Britain. At the turn of the century, America had been increasing in her anointing and, though far from perfect, became the beneficiary of Great Britain's loss. Now it seems that America is at *her* moment of truth. Specifically, I believe the glory of the Spirit of God is in the process of leaving the nations generally and, in particular, America, and moving to Israel as the spiritual head of the nations. Philadelphia, the birthplace of the nation founded on faith in Jesus, the very cradle of liberty, is the seat of America's glory. Philadelphia was the nation's first capital and the place of William Penn's grand experiment in Brotherly Love. I believe God is unstopping the well of His love that was long ago dug here. I also believe that this brotherly love is going to be experienced in Philadelphia and the nations and move from the Church to Israel. I feel that this archway of glory represents the joining of the glory of God from Philadelphia (in the nations) to Jerusalem, the capital of God's kingdom and the only place on earth where God has agreed He will set His great Name. Jerusalem is where Messiah *Yeshua* (Jesus) will rule on earth for a thousand years.

Ultimately the glory of God will rest there fully and exclusively, but prior to the Millennial Kingdom of Messiah this glory will shift increasingly to Jerusalem. And so America, and all the nations, must either cooperate with God's eternal plan or rage against it, as prophesied in Psalm 2. The Ruth portion of the Church will willingly yield the leadership in the anointing, as well as in the Olive Tree paradigm of faith in Jesus, even to the point of becoming Jewish again. The challenge for the Church is significant: remain in contact spiritually with Jerusalem and the Jewish people or lose contact with God's glory altogether. The Ruth portion of the Church will agree to this, but the rest of the Church (Orpah) will not. Those churches and leaders who refuse will most likely decrease their anointing. Those who gladly agree will be greatly blessed.

Recently God sent me another one of those coincidences to help me understand this point. A dear pastor friend of mine, John Harris, stopped in my office. As we began to talk about the Lord, he started to tell me that the Lord showed him that judgment on the Church is near; that many leaders were going to have their sins exposed; and that *ichabod*, or departed glory, would be pronounced by God over their churches. He shared that these churches were like Eli, who refused to discipline his sons, and the glory departed.

I believe this is true. How churches respond to the opportunity to bless the Jewish people will increasingly become the defining issue regarding the increase or decrease of the anointing of the Holy Spirit for every church. Unity of the various churches in each city across racial and denominational lines will be a big factor in maintaining and experiencing increase in the anointing of God's Spirit, but I believe such unity will be accomplished in those places where the principle of blessing the Jewish people is respected. In those cities, there will be great unity as Messianic Jewish believers join in with churches and the "commanded blessing" that God places on unity of the brethren is released (see Ps. 122). Churches in these cities will be key models to other cities, encouraging them to live the gospel in the face of pressure from the persecution of both Jews and Christians.

Those who refuse will be like Eli: Though he judged Israel for forty years and enjoyed blessing, his offspring grew sinful as he ministered with a slack hand. Eli was cursed because he honored his sons above God. He allowed his personal interests to become an idol, which meant more to him than serving God diligently and fully—much like Saul, but unlike Abraham, who was willing to put God above the very life of his son. The Church that is living for self will progress to blatant sins like Hophni and Phineas, Eli's sons, who began taking offerings that belonged to God. They eventually proceeded into debauchery, and the glory of God departed.

The Orpah portion of the Church , like Eli's sons, will be in no condition to help a persecuted Jewish people. She will be tempted to act like the rest of the world, determined to take Israel's heritage. Orpah will be caught in the lifestyle of the world, stained by its selfishness, unable to yield herself to God's purposes. Orpah returned to Moab, to its people and its gods. Orpah's loss of contact with Israel was a loss of God's glory as well. Only the Ruth portion of the Church will be able to remain connected to the glory of God that is returning to Israel. She will be lavishly blessed and share in Israel's glory as an equal partner. As she pours out the mercy God has given her upon the Jewish people, she will be enabling the shift of glory to Jerusalem to be accomplished. She will not feel that she has lost something, but rather gained. Just as Ruth (the Church) laid her child Obed (worship and service to God) in Naomi's (Israel's) bosom, the blessing of Naomi unto the miraculous nursing of Obed was not a loss for Ruth, but a source of great blessing. Love such as this knows only increase, never decrease. There is one who withholds and suffers lack, but there is one who gives and increases all the more (see Prov. 11:24).

Isaiah speaks to the Gentiles at the close of his prophetic book. No doubt he is referring to the millennial reign of the Messiah from Jerusalem, but I believe he's also speaking about the increasing glory of the Spirit in Jerusalem in these last days prior to Jesus' return:

> Rejoice with Jerusalem, and be glad with her, all you who love her; rejoice for joy with her, all you who mourn for her; that you may feed and *be satisfied with the consolation of her bosom*, that you may drink deeply and be delighted with the abundance of her glory. For thus says the Lord: Behold, I will extend peace to her like a river, and the *glory of the Gentiles like a flowing stream*. Then you shall feed; on her sides shall you be carried, and be dandled on her knees. As one whom his mother comforts, so I will comfort you, and you shall be comforted in Jerusalem. (Isa. 66:10–13, emphasis added)

I find it interesting that the nations are urged to drink from the breast of Jerusalem and be comforted and delighted with the "abundance of her glory." This is reminiscent of Naomi's miraculous nursing of Obed. And see that the stream of glory of the Gentiles flows to Jerusalem. The fact that comfort is being offered to the nations, gives the impression that it's going to be a long, hard time of persecution that Gentile Christians will endure during Jacob's trouble.

These verses are a beautiful turnabout of Isaiah's earlier message to Israel in chapter 60:

> Arise, shine, for your light has come! And the glory of the Lord is risen upon you. For you light has come! And the glory of the Lord is risen upon you. For behold, the darkness shall cover the earth, and deep darkness the people; but the Lord will arise over you, and His glory will be seen upon you. The Gentiles shall come to your light, and kings to the brightness of your rising. Lift up your eyes all around, and see: they all gather together,

they come to you; your sons shall come from afar, and your daughters shall be nursed at your side. Then you shall see and become radiant, and your heart shall swell with joy; because the abundance of the sea shall be turned to you, the wealth of the Gentiles shall come to you. . . . The sons of foreigners shall build up your walls, and their kings shall minister to you; for in My wrath I struck you, but in My favor I have had mercy on you. Therefore your gates shall be open continually; they shall not be shut day or night, that men may bring to you the wealth of the Gentiles, and their kings in procession, for the nation and kingdom which will not serve you shall perish, and those nations shall be utterly ruined. . . . And the sons of those who afflicted you shall come bowing to you, and all those who despised you shall fall prostrate at the soles of your feet; and they shall call you The City of the Lord, Zion of the Holy One of Israel. Whereas you have been forsaken and hated, so that no one went through you, I will make you an eternal excellence, a joy of many generations. You shall drink the milk of the Gentiles, and milk the breast of kings; you shall know that I, the Lord, am your Savior and your Redeemer, the Mighty One of Jacob. (Isa. 60:1–5, 10–12, 14–16)

The glory is brought to Israel by the Church as she shows the mercy she was shown by God (Rom. 11:31), and then the mercy results in abundance of glory as God multiplies it back to those of the Church who rejoice with Jerusalem. First, Israel in Isaiah 60 nurses at the Church's breast; and then, in Isaiah 66, the nations nurse at Israel's breast.

"O the depth of the riches both of the wisdom and the knowledge of God!" (Rom. 11:33).

CHAPTER 10

A CHURCH THAT
KNOWS ONE THING

The greatest obstacles for the Church to act with overpowering love for Israel are yokes of pride and criticism. We all struggle with these sins, which so easily beset
us. I believe the victory in these areas will come when the
Body of the Messiah returns to focusing on her common
single strength: the blood of Jesus.

For too long believers have focused on too many other
things—things that separate us. Differences in doctrine. Differences in worship. Differences in interpretation. Differences in looks, speech, tradition, liturgy. Differences, differences. Anything the devil can use to get us criticizing,
accusing, and condemning one another. We have got to
stop doing the Accuser's job for him and get back to agreeing on the one thing that will paralyze the devil and em-
power the church to fulfill her calling: unity around the
cross and the blood of our precious Lamb. That's where we

were born again. That's where we are healed and set free. It's the message of all revivals, all outpourings of the Holy Spirit. It's where we get into one place and one accord. It's got to be what the 120 in the upper room in Jerusalem were in one accord about in the Book of Acts. They had just witnessed the crucifixion and could think and talk of nothing else. We need to do the same. And we'll never be the same.

Paul told the Corinthians:

> And I, brethren, when I came to you, did not come with excellence of speech or of wisdom declaring to you the testimony of God. For I determined not to know anything among you except Jesus the Messiah and Him crucified. I was with you in weakness, in fear, and in much trembling. And my speech and my preaching were not with persuasive words of human wisdom, but in demonstration of the Spirit and of power, that your faith should not be in the wisdom of men but in the power of God. (1 Cor. 2:1–5)

Accordingly, when the Israelites left Egypt, Psalm 105:37 tells us not one was weak or feeble out of several million people. Why? They were all focused on the blood of the lamb that they had put on their doors, which saved them and set them free from slavery in Egypt.

We need to stop knowing so many things and start knowing the one thing we all agree on: that we were set free by the loving sacrifice of our wonderful Jesus, Who came and died a criminal's death to pour out the love of God on us so we could live for others and not ourselves. The Church is a body. But its parts don't communicate with one another because we've stopped communicating the only language we *all* understand: the blood of Jesus. It's the only thing we all can say "amen" to. We have to fight the temptation to think about each other in all the ways we've been thinking and just say, "praise God, you're my brother or sister, and I'm going to bring a good report about you." We can do this because the blood of Jesus has washed us clean from our sins and mistakes.

Back in the Garden of Eden, God told Satan that the seed of the woman (Jesus) was going to crush his head. He also said that Satan would bruise His heel. Little did Satan realize that these two things would happen at the same time. When Jesus' blood flowed, Satan's power and work was crushed, as all sin was paid for by His sinless blood. We must take the power of that act of love, forgiveness, and mercy residing in Jesus' blood and center our lives and ministries around it. Satan now knows how destructive that blood is for him, and he vehemently opposes the very mention of it. But it is our greatest weapon, and we dare not forget it nor neglect it. Without proclaiming it we are powerless to crush Satan's work in our lives and the lives of others. Every time Satan rears his head we must crush it again and again by proclaiming Jesus' act of love in shedding His blood to destroy Satan's every stronghold and tactic.

If we will take the blood of forgiveness and do this by forgiving others, we will not feel the need to grumble and criticize each other. We will see our real enemy is not people, and we will work toward helping others to be set free. The Church must overcome this huge obstacle if she will be a discerning, loving Ruth. Otherwise, she will be a worldly Orpah.

I'm reminded of the parable in Matthew 18:23–35 of the man who was forgiven a massive debt by his creditor, which is the equivalent of the many sins we are forgiven by God. But, when this debtor is owed a very small debt by *his*

99

debtor, he refuses to forgive it. This is what we do when we hold things against others in unforgiveness. The sobering part of this parable is that the original creditor (representing God) becomes angry that his original debtor would not act like Him and forgive the debt, and so He declared that the original massive debt was once again due.

This has serious ramifications for us. God has stated quite clearly that we are forgiven as we forgive others (see Matt. 6:14–15). And to him who shows no mercy, none will be shown by God. We must forgive; holding wrongs is not an option for us who want to remain in God's family. We *must* bring a good report. Do you know how many of the adult Israelites who left Egypt entered the Promised Land? Two! Joshua and Caleb, the ones who brought a good report. Of course, if we are still troubled by a brother who has wronged us, we may have to go to the person who has hurt us; but we must find a way to show mercy and forgiveness, and hopefully sooner rather than later. We all make mistakes. The only people who don't make mistakes are the ones who don't do or say anything. And that's a mistake. So we're all guilty before God and need mercy and forgiveness.

Without mercy, the Church will remain a dysfunctional body due to her wounds. As a body, the Church's heart has issues with the lungs, and the lungs do things differently from the kidneys, and the liver is too this or that. And as groups of believers we've remained sickly and weak and divided, and any body that is divided isn't going anywhere.

As individuals, we're wounded as well. Because we've been wounded in growing up we don't help each other enough, and though we've been saved we stay wounded. The thief comes not but to steal, to kill, and destroy; and, if we're not under the shadow of God's wing, when the thief comes he steals and wounds. We were designed by God to live for others, but we've all been wounded. Most of us are trying to survive our wounds to such an extent that we focus on our wounds and have precious little focus on bringing Jesus' blood to the healing of someone else's wounds. We need to get out of ourselves and help someone else.

I know for myself that, as a young boy of four or five, I was wounded, too. I found out that people die, and it really scared me. All of a sudden my storybook life wasn't perfect anymore, and I felt like I had a huge problem: that life was too serious. By the time I was seven years old I had already been so worried about dying that I knew I had to find God. I was taught that when we died, we just went out of existence. That seemed so wrong to me. Somehow I just knew if I could find Him, the fear and cruelty of going out of existence in seventy or eighty years would be resolved. So I decided I was going to make finding God my main goal in life.

In the process of trying to survive this overwhelming fear, I had to think, think, think about everything so I could figure this big problem out. I became so self-centered, in an effort to try to heal this wound from the devil, that I became of little help to others. While I was involved in an eternity-threatening struggle, selfishness had taken over my personality, and the Lord had to break the habits of self-centered defensiveness in me *long* after I was saved. He's still doing it.

I believe I'm not that different from the rest of those who trust in Jesus. We've all been wounded by the enemy in a myriad of ways—every time he came around and we didn't have God's armor on. Some of us were abused as children by a parent, relative, teacher or someone's boyfriend. Others were told they weren't good enough or smart enough or pretty enough or athletic enough. Whatever it was that overwhelmed us and caused us to defend our ego out of self-preservation triggered the flow of our soulish defense mechanisms. These defense mechanisms cause us to protect our self-image from all "attackers." These attackers may simply be the people in our lives. If we are defensive as a result of wounds, we may defend ourselves by criticizing others so we feel more important. Or we may boast about ourselves or our achievements so others will be impressed. Or we may complain constantly about the circumstances that come our way, in an unconscious effort to express how important we are and how unjust it is for such and such to happen to someone like us.

But Jesus said, "In the world you *shall* have tribulation, but be of good cheer, for I have overcome the world" (John 16:33). Whatever our wounded condition, Jesus has overcome it by His blood; and He's living in our spirit ready to be the Answer for it and to be released in us, to overcome for us and through us to make us a blessing to others and to our Heavenly Father. The Overcomer is in us, glory be to God! We need to let Him overcome.

Our *will* is the mechanism that decides whether to open the door of our selfish, carnal *soul* in self-defense and self-preservation with a negative report of pride or criticism (which builds our own ego); or to open the door of our loving *heart* and release a faithful response so that the Spirit of God, Who lives in our heart, can build God's kingdom as our heart's door opens.

I see it like Figure 1, below, which is not drawn with accuracy but illustrates how the will chooses a power source of either the fleshly soul or the spirit (heart). In each situation in life, the will opens up to one of the two, immediately closing off to the other.

102

Figure 1

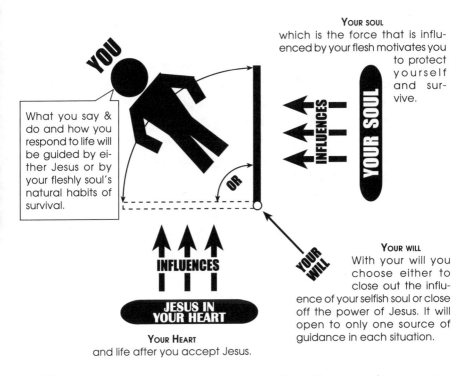

YOUR SOUL which is the force that is influenced by your flesh motivates you to protect yourself and survive.

INFLUENCES

YOUR SOUL

What you say & do and how you respond to life will be guided by either Jesus or by your fleshly soul's natural habits of survival.

OR

INFLUENCES

JESUS IN YOUR HEART

YOUR WILL

YOUR HEART and life after you accept Jesus.

YOUR WILL With your will you choose either to close out the influence of your selfish soul or close off the power of Jesus. It will open to only one source of guidance in each situation.

When we receive Jesus into our hearts and lives, the power to overcome every area of wounded-ness, need, and hunger is within us.

If we look to and trust the Lord, He will be released and will complete all the work that needs to be done in and through us.

However, because we have practiced self-preservation for most of our lives,we have established habits we think will help us survive each challenge to our wellbeing. Our soul motivates us to continue these habits and preserve ourselves.

God desires to heal these habits and for us to trust Him to protect us and not our self-promoting ego.

By our Will we will choose to die to or shut off our natural self-preserving response and seek the Lord, or to shut out the Lord and allow our soul's natural habits of survival to operate.

When the will chooses to open the soul door of self, as it opens it covers the Spirit and hides the light of Jesus within us. Jesus warned us in Matthew 5:15 that men do not light a candle and put it under a bushel, yet when we bring a negative report such as, "Here comes John. Why is he so this or that?" we are hiding the light of God's fire in our heart with the open door of the selfish soul. By criticizing we make ourselves feel better and possibly feel more righteous but we seal off the spirit, which is where our overcoming Lord resides, the One Who is waiting to show *His* character instead of our own.

Solomon tells us in Proverbs 4:23 to guard our heart "with all diligence, for *out of it* are [flow] the issues of life." The concern for guarding our heart is not that something bad might get *into* it, but rather from blocking what should flow *out* of it, namely, our Lord and the issues, or flows, that bring life. The selfish soul, influenced by our carnal desires, brings a flow of death or separation from God. Once the Spirit of God is in our heart I believe the devil doesn't *want* to get in there! The Spirit of God would cast him out and bruise him. Spiritual warfare is primarily for control of the *mind*. We must guard from covering our heart with the door of the soul, preventing the issues of life from flowing out. These issues of life are nothing less than the life of God pouring out of us to heal others and heal situations with God's nature of loving mercy released through our words and deeds of love, joy, and peace and the fruit of the Spirit.

We all need to have God's grace to break the grip of our fleshly soul, to stop living for ourselves and start living for others. We were created to be broken in soul, with our soul yielding to our spirit so we can help others fulfill their destinies. Jesus has taken up residence in us to do this very thing. But as we remain in our old, selfish patterns of behavior which we fashioned to survive our wounds, we live under the influence of our soul instead of our spirit where God's love resides. As we bring an evil report about others, the door of our soul opens to dominate our mind and the door of our heart is covered and shut. If we yield to Jesus living in us, we are able to bring the good report, thinking on what is lovely and of virtue in others (Phil. 4:8). Only then does our spirit open and God's spirit is released, first onto our own mind, and then life comes out to others. These selfish ways of pride and criticism are the yokes of bondage that God is breaking in us to set us free and to make us a blessing.

The outpouring of God's grace (that has already begun and is increasing) is going to set the Church, and us as individuals, free from selfishness, division, and criticism. God says in Isaiah 58 that this is the fast that He has chosen. I believe this is the prophetic word to the Church in this hour. This is what revivals do; the blood of Jesus is focused upon. The Holy Spirit bears witness of the blood (Heb. 10:15). He shows His approval by manifesting His presence, and we are changed and the world is changed.

And the greatest revival ever is now underway. In Acts 4:34–35, the multitude of believers sold their properties and laid the money at the apostles' feet to distribute according to the needs of others. Love and compassion were ruling over selfishness. We're going to see an outpouring greater than at Pentecost. The latter rain and former rain are being poured out at the same time on the Church. Love and compassion for a lost and dying world will flow as never before.

Clearly one of the ingredients in this anointing of the Holy Spirit will be a love for the Jewish people caught in the time of Jacob's trouble. The Ruth part of the church will be able to resist the evil report that the world brings about the Jewish people. The world, through the influences of the evil one, will want to destroy Israel and the Jewish people. But God, through the anointing of the Holy Spirit, will break the yokes of bondage in each true believer, so that the Ruth portion of the church will be like God—selfless and generous and living for others, the way we were intended to be. She will have a good report about Jews and Israel on her lips. It will be dangerous, but glorious. Our Lord is returning for such a glorious, loving, spotless bride, who is able to apply Jesus' blood to her own wounds and also to the wounds of others.

CHAPTER 11

STORIES OF SOME
CALLED TO HELP JEWS

It's usually good to take principles and theories that dwell in the ivory tower and bring them down to the practical highways and byways of earth. If the thoughts that I've shared in this book are from God, others will be thinking, feeling, and believing them as well. I'm aware that there will be opposition to a book that tells of things not happening before our eyes; that's human nature, and that's spiritual warfare. Unless God prevents it, some will surely challenge the assertions I've presented in my usual doesn't-everybody-think-this-way? fashion.

But in an effort to move from the theory to the practical, I have set aside this chapter to give you a sampling of people who have shared with me their own thoughts and feelings and impressions from the Lord about helping Jewish people in what they believe to be a coming time of persecution. If there are future printings of this book I hope to

107

increase the number of stories from people whom God has instructed to do wonderful things like you will now read about. I know there are many others, but these will demonstrate that God is surely on the move on behalf of His Church and His ancient Jewish people. For reasons of security I do not disclose names or precise places. This has been the request of each of the following people who did not want their future effectiveness compromised.

MIDWEST

I am a homemaker from a rural area in the Midwestern United States. About twenty-five years ago I watched an interview on television with Corrie ten Boom. I watched in awe as she described her testimony of hiding Jews during the Holocaust and how she and her family were arrested. I did not understand what motivated her and her family to literally give their lives for a people, most of them strangers. But her love and devotion to the Jewish people made an indelible mark on my heart.

A few years later I met an Orthodox Jewish family from Israel who had come to America to encourage Jewish people to emigrate to Israel. We became good friends. He was not a believer in Jesus. He taught me from the Old Covenant. I began to see I believed in the Jewish Messiah, the God of Abraham, Isaac, and Jacob. He also challenged me with troublesome questions of the church's history and interpretation of Scriptures that were anti-Semitic.

At one point we invited him and his family to our home in the country for a weekend of relaxation. The first night began the Jewish Sabbath, and so we prepared for this beautiful festival. As my friend set the traditional *challah* bread

on the table, without explanation he began to sprinkle Ko-
sher salt on the *challah*. I realized he was making a covenant of salt between our families, a lifetime commitment
to us. God had been showing me about this covenant of
salt, and I wept at his willingness to stand with us so deeply,
though we were Gentiles.

With these seeds the Holy Spirit began to do something
in my heart. One night alone with the Lord about twenty
years ago I got on my knees and made a covenant with God
that I would be forever aligned with the Jewish people and
Israel. I would go where they would go, stay where they
stay. They would be my people and their God would be my
God, just as Ruth said (Ruth 1:16–17). As I wept, I knew
that I may be called to die for or with my new family, the
Jewish people. I also knew God wanted me to comfort His
people (Isa. 40:1).

Since then I have taught the Jewish roots of the faith
to hundreds of Christians who mistakenly believed that
the church replaced Israel and exclusively owns her blessings. I have worked within Jewish organizations against
hate groups, fearing for my very life from threats made
against me.

I have seen many Gentile believers in Jesus (*Yeshua*)
make a covenant of sacrifice for the Jewish people. They
share some unique feelings. One is a longing for Israel, a
sense that they currently reside in a country that is not their
own. Some have visited Israel and actually mourned when
they had to leave. Another is a hunger for the Jewishness of
their faith and the delight of discovering the Jewish feasts
(Lev. 23) and their significance. Some have a pervasive, almost nagging sense of "where could I hide Jews in time of

persecution?" I too have experienced this with every home I move to.

I believe making such a covenant is very serious but very dear in God's heart. If you are ready, get on your knees and tell the Lord "*Hineni.*" That's what the prophets have said to him: "Here am I."

SOUTHEAST

I am a pastor of thirty years from the Southeastern part of America. I lived in a certain city for sixty-five years. Imagine my surprise when in 1988 a man with a prophetic gift pointed right at me and said, "You're leaving this city! You're moving a hundred miles from here to a rural area," and he described several characteristics about the place where I now live. Years after this prophecy (I had actually forgotten it) I bought a piece of property as an investment. Later I checked my car's odometer, and it was exactly one hundred miles from my home. It had some cabins on it, but mostly it was just rural land.

One night I was sleeping in one of the cabins when I had three dreams in the same night. In the first dream the Lord showed me that the larger house I had been building on the property would be used for evangelism. In the second dream, there were groups of people who came to the large house on my land. I could read their hearts. The Lord spoke to me in the dream and said to me: "Take care of my people."

In the third dream, I saw hundreds of people walking down the road to this large house on my land. I was alarmed at how many people were coming, and I said to the Lord, "We don't have enough room for all these people!"

The Lord spoke to me, saying: "They've not come to stay; they've come to pass."

In this dream the verse from Luke 24:52 came into my mind. It's after Jesus' resurrection and ascension when those whom he had led to Bethany watched Him ascend. It says there, "And they worshiped Him and returned to Jerusalem with great joy."

I know that many people will be coming to my property. I also know they are Jews who will be persecuted. They will stay with us for a short time on their way back to their homeland, Israel. They will hear about their Messiah at our place of safe haven. And they will return to Jerusalem worshiping Him with great joy.

SOUTH #1

I am a businesswoman living in the deep South. I am an intercessor who prays much for the Jewish people. The Lord has been speaking to me about a time of persecution coming on the Jewish people in America and my role during that time. I have a close and intimate relationship with Him, which I believe is going to become ever more crucial in the days ahead. I would like to share a word I believe the Lord has spoken to me during a time of prayer. It was spoken to me through a prayer partner on March 29, 1996, and I submit excerpts for those who hear it to discern for themselves if they sense it is from the Lord. I believe it is and that the Lord is preparing me and others to provide refuge for Jewish people on their way to Israel:

The Lord would say that even in these next few weeks and months what I'm going to do is I'm going to give you revelation even of the understanding of the Jewish traditions of My people and I'm going to even teach you the Hebrew roots of your Christianity; and even as you do, you're going to come into a fresh revelation of understanding of the Messiah, even *Yeshua Hamashiach*.

The Lord would say you are going to come to even understand the basis of the foundation of the roots of Christianity, which is going to be important for you even in evangelism. The Lord would say that I'm going to take your home at the right season. It will be a refuge even for the Jews. I'm not going to give you one home but I'm going to give you many homes. The Lord would say that that's the Prophet's reward coming upon your life. The Lord would say that now I draft you even in real estate for Myself. Not only in real estate for the world, but I'm going to draft you into building places and the refuge homes and the hostel homes where My people will even find a place of refuge in the time when anti-Semitism will rise up against them in the nation, and the nation will attempt to destroy them. But you will have a place—you will even have an underground. You will have an underground networking that will network the people back to their land.

I will even give you the availability to the airlines. The Lord would say I'm going to give you someone even in the airlines who is going to be able to open the door even in the season. I'm going to give you a relationship there; and even as I do, it is going to provide an opening for you that you will have the availability to even take My people from this nation even to send them back into their nation, back to Israel. The Lord would say that truly as you have prayed for the peace of Jerusalem, NOW the Lord would say that even the blessings of Jerusalem come upon your life. The Lord would say that the Prophet's reward moves upon you even now. It is the blessing of

Israel, the blessing of Jerusalem. For truly you have been called as one who is going to be able to bring refuge to My people in the day in which they need it. The Lord would say that you will be a general to an army of My covenant people. You will be one who will be commanded even by Me, and even as I release the commands you will give those commands and provide a way in which for My covenant people to return even unto their land. I will even give you the instructions; I will even give you the battle plan; I will give you even everything necessary in that hour. The Lord would say, Think not lightly of the calling. For you will be a witness even unto the Jewish nation. (God has given you a number of pieces of land and homes, and there's a networking, and I see a tunnel that is important.)

AUTHOR'S NOTE: I have spoken with many people who believe that there will be an underground railroad-type situation in America, similar to the way that African Americans escaped slavery in the South more than a hundred years ago. The next story that I relate is also from the South, and this woman also feels impressed in her spirit that this is true.

South #2

I have known Jesus since I was seven years old. God gave me a love for the Old Testament as a young girl. I found it clear when others did not. I would study Jewish things and not fit in with others, but I believe God was setting me apart to be given to His ancient Jewish people. God continued to give me a close relationship with Him and call me His "daughter of Zion" in times with Him. I felt as if He was just letting me know I was special to Him until about two years ago I heard Him tell me in prayer, "Ask for the Jews." I didn't know what He meant, but I did ask. He said, "number them." So I said a number, and He said "larger." And every time He said "larger" until I reached hundreds of thousands. I knew God was calling me to intercede for the Jewish people and love them, which I do.

About six years ago my husband and I bought a piece of property where we built our home. It is situated near a slave route, where slaves were taken up north to freedom. My husband and I knew, as the Lord impressed it upon our hearts, that this property was to be used for Jews and Christians who would be persecuted. Just as slaves went north through our area, we know Jews will come south on their way to Israel. And we will hide them and help them and risk our lives if need be.

The Lord recently had me go to Jerusalem, and while there I was looking out over Jerusalem He said to me about the city, "This is the one my soul loves." He said this to me three times and told me He had planted Jerusalem as a jewel in my heart. He told me He was holding me out in His hand as a sign and a wonder to show the world what He will do with those who will just love Him. I believe that God is going to mightily bless those who love Him enough to lay down their lives for the people He loves.

God gave me a dream not long ago where there were several Orthodox Jews who came up to me and looked at me as nothing special. As I looked at them I felt they knew more than me and that I really knew very little. But I heard the Lord say in this dream, "I'm sending you to the Jews."

I responded by crying. I was overwhelmed by my inability, and I asked Him, "Why are You sending me? I know nothing."

And the Lord said, "That's exactly why I'm sending you." I can't say that I understand what God is doing in me, but I know what He's told me and the love He's put in me for the Jewish people. I am beginning to learn Hebrew now, and I am just waiting on Him.

WESTERN

The following is a letter I received in December of 1997. I reproduce it in that format without the signature:

Dear Jeff,
Shalom and warm greetings. I'm sorry it has taken a while to respond to our last conversation on the phone. Between having company staying with us and office priorities I have not gotten to it until now.

I am involved in a Christian ministry that is helping to assist Jewish people to their homeland Israel from areas in the world where there is growing persecution. In the last few years while traveling and speaking around America, it has become quite clear that God is putting a network of believers together who are preparing to assist Jewish people in a time of persecution here in the US. Many have shared their dreams, visions and scriptures which they sincerely believe to be given by the Lord, clearly directing them to prepare a place and/or transportation for Jewish people for a difficult time in the future. It seems to me that only the Holy Spirit could put together such a thing.

While traveling with my family on vacation, we felt impressed by the Lord to buy a small house fairly close to the US border. We later received confirmation from Him of its purpose for the Jewish people.

God is moving by His Spirit, pray that our ears will be open to His call! Blessings to you.
(P.S. Please do not use our name)

I have met all but one of these people who have shared their impressions, dreams, and feelings. I know the daughter of the one I did not meet. I have found them to be sensible, "normal" people, leading apparently successful lives and having a genuine love for the Lord. I believe they represent only the tip of the iceberg among many Christians who are preparing to help Jewish people in a coming time of trouble. I have additional stories that I have not shared here. The sampling of stories that I have reported are from all parts of America.

In this same vein, I recently attended a national conference in America, where providing "safe houses" for soon-to-be persecuted Jews was among the topics of discussion and was attended by approximately fifty people. I am aware of further networking that is taking place and am hearing from more people all the time who share this burden.

I believe persecution is coming soon. Something will set it in motion. At that time all that we believe and all that we are will be tested. We will need His grace like never before to act in a way that glorifies Him in the dark days that are ahead. These will also be wonderful days of miracles and wonders, which often come in troubled times, and we are to be of good cheer because He has overcome this world! Hallelujah. Even in tribulation we can praise Him. And we are surely to look up, for our redemption draws near.

CHAPTER 12

WHAT TO DO NOW

If somehow this book has been placed in your hands and you've never taken the opportunity to invite Jesus into your life, then I would urge you to do so now. (Jesus' Hebrew name is *Yeshua*; for He is a Jew, as were His disciples and, with the likely exception of Luke, so was every writer of the New Testament.) Every person has sinned or disobeyed God, and you and I are no exception. God gave us the choice to obey Him or disobey Him so that our obedience would have meaning. Obeying God leads to closeness and eternal life, while disobeying Him leads to eternal separation—which is death, or the absence of God Who is lifegiving Spirit. The good news is that God knew we would all disobey Him before we decided to obey Him, so He became a man in order to die our death for us.

Those who receive the grace to trust in this Jesus, God the Son, do not receive the punishment for their sins—which is to remain separated from Him as we've previously chosen—but instead are forgiven. They have now chosen to turn away from our sins and offer to God the Father the sacrifice of His Son in payment for our sins. That is truly good news! Jesus, like a lamb, was sacrificed, received God's anger at our sin, and thus paid for it with His death as the Passover Lamb, so we are able to receive God's loving forgiveness. We need only to trust that this is so and that, since Jesus was spotless, He could not remain separated from God the Father, but arose to Him after dying this horrible death for us. If you can repent of your sins and invite Jesus into your heart, He will enter your heart in His Spirit and dwell there and transform you to be a son or daughter of the Father like He is. Just say these, or similar, words and mean them with all your heart:

> Dear God, I'm sorry for all of my sins against You. I know I broke Your laws and I ask you to forgive me. I turn from these selfish ways and trust in Jesus' atoning death that my sins may be forgiven. I invite the living Jesus into my heart to change me and cleanse me so that I can live unto You, Father, and not for myself. I will now stop being my own master and ask you to be my Savior, Master, and Lord. I believe Your Son, Jesus, is my Lord, and I will follow His words and ways (which are Your words and ways, too) with all my heart.

If you've said this prayer, find a good church or Messianic congregation to worship each week, and grow in grace and knowledge by praying daily and reading the Bible daily. Also, please write to me. I'd love to hear from you.

If you already know your heavenly Father and feel God is calling you to help Jewish people, pray for His guidance as to how He wants you to help, and then obey Him. He may lead you to encourage other Christians to be like Ruth and not Orpah. Maybe He'll have you give this book to others or share your feelings. Be bold, but be gentle and loving. Though blessing Abraham's seed is a great source of blessing, it is also a matter of God's grace. The world has been bringing a strong negative report about the Jewish people since the first Jew, Abraham, was on the scene.

Bring a good report about the Jewish people. If you proclaim it, you'll be amazed at how people will polarize before your eyes. In this way, you'll see others who believe like you, and you can encourage each other. You'll also see believers who are influenced by the world's report, so you can pray for them to receive the grace necessary to bring a good report, help the Jewish people and themselves, and please God.

Be aware that this is not a safe message. I believe it will become increasingly dangerous to preach this message, but God is in control and He will bless you and protect you. If He leads you to set aside property or tangible goods, you need not fear. He is in control; have a giving spirit and not fear.

This is the heart of God from all the ages and before there was time. This is why God created us. He is summing up all things in His Son (Eph. 1:10).

Rejoice with the Jewish people. Moses closes his song to Israel at the end of the Torah by including the Gentiles. He says: "Rejoice, O Gentiles, with His people; for He will avenge the blood of His servants, and render vengeance to His adversaries; He will provide atonement for His land and His people." (Deut. 32:43) Be joyful over Israel's blessings and never jealous. All those who love God share in Israel's blessings. Above all, pray. Pray for yourself and others. The stakes are high, but the rewards are beyond what we could ask or think.

I will close with the priestly blessing that Aaron pronounced over Israel from Numbers 6:

> The Lord bless you and keep you; the Lord make His face shine upon you, and be gracious to you; the Lord lift up His countenance upon you, and give you peace. (Num. 6:24–26)

In the name of our Prince of Peace. Amen! In this way God placed His name on the children of Israel so they belonged to Him. Let Him do the same for you. I believe this blessing embodies all the principles of this book. God has spoken a blessing over all He chooses, ordaining us into eternal life. Then He keeps us and watches over us. He orders our circumstances to bring forth fruit in our lives. Wonderfully, He makes the shining face of Jesus (*Yeshua*) shine in our hearts and changes our very nature to be like His. This is our salvation, and it is done by grace—by unmerited favor. Then the Lord takes that glorious treasure within us and lifts it up to illuminate our minds to overcome every obstacle and transform our selfish ways of self-preservation, giving us peace so we can be a blessing to others. In effect, the Light of the World makes us the light of the world. And if we follow through and bless others, the light in us will never go out, but shine with the glory of God. I have prayed that this blessing would come on every person who reads this book, in the Name of our Prince of Peace. Amen!

EPILOGUE

I know that God has called me as a Jew to speak to the
nations. Since I first believed in *Yeshua* (Jesus) back in
1974, nothing has thrilled me more than the love I've seen
in so many Christians for the Jewish people. I have written
The Last Chance to encourage and strengthen that love and
to give it a Biblical and prophetic framework, so that it may
flourish.

I have spoken with many Christians who feel something in their hearts for Israel, Jews, and Jewishness, but
do not know why or even what they are feeling. I trust this
little book will help to explain what God is doing in them.

I truly believe God is doing this today as one of His
most important acts on our behalf. Not every Christian will
be able to provide shelter and material needs to the Jewish
people in the coming time of Jacob's trouble. But every
Christian is able to pray. God instructs us in Psalm 122 to
pray for the peace of Jerusalem. It says there that those who
do so shall prosper. So I urge you to pray as never before

for the City of Peace and the weary people God has entrusted it to for His purposes. I urge you to allow God to fan into flame a love for the Jewish people that will help fulfill their destiny and your own.

In the final days before Jesus' return, every nation, tribe, and tongue will be attempting to have Jerusalem for their very own, but it belongs to the people who are Abraham's seed. In this age, that means Abraham's physical descendants and those from the nations who are one with her. Ultimately, Jerusalem shall descend from heaven and be comprised of living stones, every true believer for whom Jesus has shed His sinless blood, the true bride of the Messiah, both Gentile and Jew.

To order additional copies of

The Last Chance
For the Church to Love
the Jewish People

send $9.95 plus $3.95 shipping and handling to:

Books, Etc.
PO Box 1406
Mukilteo, WA 98275

or have your credit card ready and call:

(800) 917-BOOK

You may contact the author by writing to:
Mechaya World Ministries
PO Box 751
Bala Cynwyd, PA 19004
or by e-mail: jeff@mechaya.org